7 Words That Can Change The World

THE SIMPLE TRUTH
&
THE DEATH OF SACRED COWS*

JOSEPH R. SIMONETTA

* SACRED COW: A person, idea, custom, or institution unreasonably held to be above question, criticism, or curtailment.

Copyright © 2019 by Joseph R. Simonetta
This is a revised and expanded version of Seven Words That Can Change The World published originally by Hampton Roads Publishing Company.
All rights reserved, including the right to reproduce this work in any form whatsoever, without permission in writing from the author, except for brief passages in connection with a review.
ISBN-13: 978-1548095086
ISBN-10: 1548095087
WEB SITE: www.SevenWordsChangeTheWorld.com

DEDICATION

For my wife, Susana, and our children,
Russell and Fiorella.

OTHER BOOKS BY
Joseph R. Simonetta

*The Heroes Are Us:
A Call to Rescue Our World*

*Russell, Alexandra, and John,
A Story of Personal and Planetary Change*

*The Book of Observations,
Life on Earth*

Religion, An Obstacle to Human Progress

*The Skeptic's Book of Religious
Quotes and Anecdotes*

*ONE, A Third Millennium Belief System
(an earlier version of 7 Words)*

CONTENTS

Foreword 1

Architecture of Life 3

Part I   An Arduous Journey 11

Part II   The Problem 17

      Means Without Goals. 19

      Profit, Power, and Progress 25

      Democracy. 29

      Education. 33

      Religion 37

      Primitive Beliefs 41

Part III The Solution 47

      Context, Perspective, and Time Frames. 49

      Cosmology. 51

      Earth 57

      Science and Religion. 65

      Sacredness: A New Understanding 75

      We Advance Technologically. 75

Infancy of Our Intelligence. 77

Spiritual 81

Sacred Construct 85

Critical Mindshift. 91

Three Simple Rules. 95

The Foundational Relationships 99

The Law of One 99

Relationship With Self 103

Relationships With Others 111

Relationship With Our Environment. 113

Our Competing Sets of Survival Instincts. 117

Grounded in Reality. 123

Declaration of Humanity 129

Author   135

FOREWORD

Well, here it is. The Formula. The Answer. The Way. Of course, everyone has The Formula, The Answer, The Way. This is not the private domain of gurus on mountaintops or teachers in temples.

The guru in your heart knows The Formula. The teacher in the temple of your being has The Answer. And your soul itself is The Way.

Still, it is nice to have it articulated so brilliantly, so fluently, so directly and unambiguously as we see it here.

When I first read this material, I found myself turning the corner of a page every time I came across something that I knew I wanted to slip into my talks. I give little talks around the world on life, the meaning of existence, and the way to have it all make sense, and as I was reading Joe Simonetta's words I thought, "Wow. I can use this as a reference. This is really good."

But by the time I got finished reading I had turned down nearly every other page. I thought, "My God, I'm going to have to memorize this man's entire book."

I knew then that I had to make sure I played my role in getting it to a larger audience, because I thought, "Gosh, if I'm responding to this book in this way, so will other people."

And I was right. Every other person to whom I've shown this material has said, basically, what I said when I put it down. Which was: "Whoa. What a powerful book. Really remarkable. Elegant simplicity."

This is a totally empowering piece of writing. Do not be misled by its small size. It is just as meaningful (perhaps more so) than any five- or six-hundred-page book I have ever read.

If you are looking to help change our planet, if you are wishing to change your own life, you have just given yourself the most practical tools you will ever have. With these simple tools you will say, "I can do this. This is something I can do."

Tampa, Florida radio personality Joel Chudnow refers to the little gem of a book that you are now holding as "a thousand-page book in a hundred pages." I like that. That pretty much says it.

There are three rules of life listed here. Three rules, seven words. Those seven words can heal the world. So, I didn't have to memorize Joe's entire book after all. I only had to remember three rules, seven words.

Here they are. Seven words. A simple mantra that will work. A little secret that will renew your enthusiasm for life.

Here it is. The Formula. The Answer. The Way.

One formula. One answer. One way. There are others, of course. We all know that. There is more than one path to paradise.

But this path is so simple. So practical. So easy.

It allows us to come to a new understanding of sacredness without all the trappings of some other approaches—without years of study and meditation, without rituals to perform and masters to follow, without classes or workshops or seminars, without, well, much effort at all.

Which is how it should be, it has always seemed to me. Truth should be a simple thing.

So here it is. The Simple Truth. Enjoy.

And pass it on.

Neale Donald Walsch

ARCHITECTURE OF LIFE

When I was a candidate for the United States Congress from Pennsylvania's 15th Congressional District, after I won the Democratic Party's nomination in the 1986 primary election, a professor from Lehigh University said to me, "You know, you are liable to win this election; you're trying something different. You're telling the truth."

As it turned out, the fifth-term incumbent Republican congressman whom I challenged and who outspent me nine to one—I refused to seek or accept PAC money—won in the general election.

I received forty-three percent of the vote, more than any previous challenger.

As a complete unknown at the start of my campaign, I had worked hard for and achieved the name recognition that would have enabled me to launch another challenge two years later.

When that time came, however, I decided not to run for office again.

From my seventeen-month, nonstop political campaign, I developed a keen understanding of the world of politics.

The answers to our problems, I learned, would never come from that battleground of adversarial self-interest groups.

Larger issues and realities must first be understood and resolved in order for the political process to serve the common good.

The "simple truths" in this book address those larger problems.

These problems are complex, severe, and compounded by the fact that *we add about 1,500,000 people to our population weekly.*

When we see and experience great injustice, suffering, inequity, and violence daily, we want desperately to solve such problems.

But how?

How can we reduce ignorance and suffering and expand knowledge and justice?

Where do we begin?

As Albert Einstein observed, we can't solve our problems from the same level of thinking out of which they originated.

What level of thinking are we at? What level must we get to?

How do we get there?

Journalist Edward R. Morrow once said, "The obscure we see eventually, the completely apparent takes a little longer."

Curious statement, "the completely apparent takes a little longer." Mark Twain, commenting about life, said similarly, "What tedious training day after day, year after year, never ending to learn common sense."

"The completely apparent."

"Common sense."

As we grow older, we learn that common sense is not that common.

Common sense to an uncommon degree is what the world calls wisdom.

Wisdom about what? Wisdom about life.

About the architecture of life.

That is what this book is about: *the architecture of life.*

At 50 years old, I earned a Master of Divinity degree in 1993 from Harvard Divinity School.

I also attended Yale Divinity School (1990-1991). I transferred my Yale credits to Harvard.

After studying the world's religions objectively at Harvard, I was struck by the fact that there was really nothing there.

This will come as a shock to most readers.
Others who have studied similarly will nod in agreement.

Yes, of course, there is all the history and the rituals, music, costumes, and theatre associated with religion.
It's a rich tapestry.
But it is all very antiquated.
It's an abundant amount of nonsense concocted in the infancy of our intelligence that should be acknowledged as such.

In the third year of the Master of Divinity program at Harvard each student was required to write a senior thesis.
Two semesters were devoted to it.
It was taken very seriously.
During one of the seminar sessions for our senior thesis, the professor asked each student to tell the class the subject of his or her thesis.
When it was my turn to speak, I said I would write about the need for a new world belief system.
My statement, to say the least, startled a number of my classmates.

In the fall semester of 1992 and spring semester of 1993, my last semesters at Harvard, I wrote a manuscript entitled, *One, A Third Millennium Belief System.*
I used parts of my manuscript for my senior thesis.
I had completed my thesis early enough in the spring semester to allow me time to work on other required final papers and study for a number of final exams.

Unexpectedly, I got a call from my senior thesis professor.
He asked that I meet in his office with him and another professor.
At the meeting, I was informed that my thesis was unacceptable.
If I wanted to write a thesis like I wrote, they said I would have to contrast my ideas with those of noted theologians.

They could have told me this long before this meeting as they were aware fully of my subject matter.

It was about three weeks before graduation.

They said I would not graduate but I could come back the next year and try again.

This was devastating news.

I had worked extremely hard for three years at Yale and Harvard. I felt blindsided.

While at that meeting with those two professors, they explained that I would have to read numerous books in order to write the kind of paper they wanted.

They provided me with a long list of the titles of these books.

They said that, if I wanted, in the next academic year, I could read these books and write and submit a new thesis.

I took a look at their list.

I said that I would read those books immediately, write a new paper, and submit it for consideration to be accepted so I could graduate with my class.

They did not believe I could do this but agreed to let me try.

I went from that meeting to the Harvard Divinity School library.
I got the books.
I read and skimmed them all.
If they wanted a conventional thesis paper, I could do that.
I'd already written many such papers at Yale and Harvard and while I studied years earlier for my Master of Architecture degree at the University of Colorado.

I wrote a new thesis along the lines that they required. I submitted it and waited.

Concurrently, I had to write other papers and take exams at the end of the spring semester.

It was a huge challenge.
I got through it all and waited to hear if my thesis was accepted or rejected.
I got the call for which I had waited.
They accepted my new paper.
It was an enormous relief.
I graduated with my class.

During the summer of 1993, I submitted my manuscript, *One, A Third Millennium Belief System,* to numerous publishers in an effort to get it published.

I received only polite rejections if I got a response at all.
I put the manuscript aside, found a job, and went to work.

A couple of years later, I revised the manuscript and gave it a new name, *A Baby Boomer's Search for Religion (from a World War II Housing Project to Harvard Divinity School).*
As an aside, I was raised in a "World War II Housing Project."
Again, I worked on getting the manuscript published.
Again, I was unsuccessful.

In the latter part of 1997, in Sarasota, Florida, a physician friend of mine, Dr. Fred Ryersbach, asked me to speak to a gathering of people in the upscale community where he lived.
Fred, quite a bit older than me, and I used to have philosophical conversations.
Fred was very intelligent and made people think harder.
He liked and shared many of my thoughts about religion and the state of the world.

I spoke to a group of people in Fred's community.
These were mostly retired and affluent professional men and women.

They were very moved by the material that I presented and asked me to speak again.

Shortly thereafter, I spoke again to this group.

During the second session with that group, a person asked if I could speak to another group of people at a different place.

This was a pattern that repeated itself.

I would speak at one place and be asked by someone in the audience to speak at another location.

Soon, I was speaking to varied audiences across the country from Florida to California.

I entitled my talk "Astonish the World, Tell the Simple Truth." Many people asked me to publish what I spoke about.

At first, I resisted as I had already self-published several books with little success.

Years ago, it was far more difficult to get any exposure for self-published books.

Today it is different.

Nevertheless, I self-published a book which I titled *The Simple Truth, A New Understanding of Sacredness*.

This was now the third name, but would not be the last, given to the manuscript that I wrote in my last year at Harvard Divinity School.

As noted, in 1986 in Pennsylvania, I was the Democratic Party nominee for the U.S. House of Representatives for PA's 15th Congressional District.

Having heard about my political background, a representative of the Natural Law Party in 2000 asked me to be their nominee from Florida, where I then lived, for the U.S. Senate.

The Natural Law Party was one of the "third parties," not a major U.S. political party like the Democrats or Republicans.

Dr. John Hagelin, a Harvard Ph.D. physicist was their candidate for the U.S. presidency.

At first, aware of how third party candidates were largely ignored by the press, I said that I was not interested.
I thought about it more and decided to accept their offer and take on the challenge.
I formed a campaign committee and we went to work.
My core message was campaign finance reform.
I planned to speak in all of Florida's major cities.

I announced my candidacy at an event in Sarasota, Florida.
John Hagelin, the presidential candidate, was there.
Both he and I gave moving and very well-received talks.
About 400 people attended the event and reception which was held in a beautiful Sarasota establishment.
The press was notified properly but none showed up.
It was a harbinger of things to come.

My campaign held its first rally outdoors in downtown Sarasota near the public library.
Hundreds attended.
I spoke on the need for campaign finance reform.
With flags and signs, we marched through Sarasota's downtown streets.
There was no press coverage although, again, they were notified properly.
The same non-coverage occurred in other cities in Florida where I spoke.

I attended the Natural Law Party's national convention near Washington, D.C.
The *New York Times* best-selling author, Neale Donald Walsch, an enthusiastic supporter of the Natural Law Party, attended the convention.

— *7 Words That Can Change the World* —

In a conversation with Neale, I offered him a copy of my self-published book, *The Simple Truth*, which he accepted graciously.

About a week later at home in Sarasota, I got phone call from Neale.

He said he read my book, *The Simple Truth,* on the plane when he flew back to his home in Oregon.

He explained that he gave talks all over the world.

When he read my book, he said that he turned the corner of the page when he found something he could use in his talks.

When he finished *The Simple Truth*, he had turned the corner of nearly every other page.

While the book, he said, *was* the simple truth as titled, he recommended that the name of the book be changed to *Seven Words Than Can Change the World*.

I changed the name and Neale wrote the Foreword.

PART I

AN ARDUOUS JOURNEY

As a child, I wondered,
"Why do we create so many problems?

A llow me to relate to you the nature of my background. It will help you understand how I arrived at the conclusions you will find in this book.

Please grant me this indulgence.

As a child, I was disturbed by the insensitive and unkind ways we humans treat each other.

I recognized that the pattern was cruel and unsustainable.

"Why do we create so many problems?" I wondered.

"Life need not be this difficult," I thought.

At that young age, I could not understand much beyond my instinct that something was wrong.

Ahead were many roads for me to travel and much to learn.

As I experienced and observed life as a young man and later as an adult, I continued to be troubled deeply by cruel and destructive behavior that I witnessed over and over.

I was disturbed that our world is thick with suffering, inequity, injustice, and exploitation.

I was haunted without relief by how we destroy each other, our environment, and even our own bodies and minds.

I wondered how we could live amidst abundance yet simultaneously exist in a sea of anxiety, fear, insecurity, greed, and self-centeredness.

I had a desperate need to understand.

My inherent nature, contemplative and proactive, drove me into the classrooms of our world.

I recall that *I never wanted to be anything.*

I just wanted to be, to follow life's bidding.

When I think about that now, many years later, it occurs to me that was an unusual approach to life.

It was an inclination that set me up for an unpredictable, sometimes perilous, and often rewarding journey.

My curiosity and sense of adventure propelled me.

My abilities and discipline enabled and sustained me.

Circumstances and serendipity allowed me.

I became and, to this day, remain a student of life.

In my travels and experiences, I was aware of my motion but not my destination.

The latter I knew to be distant.

It would reveal itself only after an arduous journey, just as a great mountain yields its summit only after one conquers its lesser peaks.

Victories and defeats nourished and thrashed me.

I forged on in search of the common but elusive thread that weaves through and binds all relationships.

I immersed myself in rich learning experiences in a broad range of seemingly unrelated fields.

I feel as if I have lived numerous lifetimes.

Over time, external forms began to dissolve into a transparency that revealed glimpses of the underlying foundation that girds our existence.

— *Part I - An Arduous Journey* —

Clarity emerged that liberated me from much of the cultural programming to which we are subjected relentlessly.

I began to see and understand the cause and effect relationships of life.

Once clear, I was able to ask and answer some fundamental questions.

I examined our religious belief systems because, for many of us, albeit less and less, they color our observations and form the basis for our decisions that result in our actions.

I searched to discover that which is sacred.

While all religions claim to have sacred qualities, I was determined to identify those things in life, in reality, that are truly sacred.

Having exhausted my search for sacredness in the world of religions, I looked for a non-religious reality-based understanding of what is sacred: ***that in life which cannot, at our peril, be violated, damaged, dishonored or destroyed.***

Drawing on my life's experiences, and study and still more experiences as an older student at Harvard and Yale Divinity Schools, I finally found what I was after.

It is a way of relating that is not arbitrary but imperative.

It addresses the reality that everything in our world is related and that the proper manner of these relationships must be understood and practiced if we are to survive and advance as a civilization.

This manner of relating is characterized by qualities that nourish and sustain the relationships of life, as opposed to those that damage and destroy them.

It may be that which Lao Tzu refers to in the *Tao Te Ching* (The Way of Life) written twenty-six hundred years ago.

The answers are simple, elegant really, but elusive.

They have to do with what I refer to as the foundational relationships of life, "sacred" relationships.

Out of these relationships, all relationships and endeavors follow. As you read on, you will understand.

The odyssey of my life that propelled me through a labyrinth of rich and diverse educational experiences convinces me that *we humans must find a new track on which to travel.*

It is evident that there is a need for a belief system more relevant to the complex and increasingly sophisticated age in which we live, a belief system with the potential to achieve universal acceptance.

A belief system responsive to the problems of our time and capable of drawing people everywhere together.

Of most importance, a belief system that can reduce ignorance and suffering and expand knowledge and justice.

I concluded, after I spoke with many others, that there are countless people—an ever-growing number—who seek such a belief system.

While there are many who are satisfied with their present belief systems, there are at least as many who are not.

Curious to know what my fellow divinity students at Harvard thought about the need for a new belief system, I took a formal written survey of their opinions.

Most, I found, were dissatisfied and felt a need for revisions to their belief systems or desired an entirely new one that would address current issues with current knowledge.

Within the diverse survey responses of my fellow students were unifying themes.

There was a strong call for a universal belief system that would be acceptable to everyone and that would honor the dignity of each person.

There was an abiding respect for diversity that allows for and encourages both individuality and assimilation within our interdependence.

— Part I - An Arduous Journey —

There was a desire for a non-patriarchal belief system and an equitable distribution of power.

There was a desire for a belief system that is more contemporary and more relevant to life in this world.

There was a passion for social change and the elimination of inequities.

There was a wish that people around the world would develop a global sense of community that transcends the limited notion of nation-states, because we all have fundamental needs in common.

There was a call for truth and knowledge.

Resonating throughout the responses was a clarion call for recognition of the sacredness of the natural world, and that the care and respect for planet Earth is a "sacred" duty.

I was encouraged by the results of that survey.

For many years, I spent countless hours sifting through volumes of information in hallowed university halls and the not so hallowed streets of many cities searching for answers.

Now, I discovered that the answers I found and the belief system to which those answers led me addressed all of the concerns that the survey revealed, and more.

Let me take you through an overview of what I perceive to be our problem.

Following that is the architecture—the design and structure—of the solution.

PART II
THE PROBLEM

"Technological societies know how to create material wealth, but their ultimate success will depend on their ability to formulate a postindustrial humanistic culture. The shift from obsession with quantitative growth to the search for a better life will not be possible without radical changes in attitudes."

Rene Dubos, Celebrations of Life

MEANS WITHOUT GOALS

Many of us are troubled by much of what we observe and experience in life.

Increasing numbers of us seek meaning and purpose in an often impersonal, materialistic, and adversarial world.

We share a growing conviction that reconciliation among people, nations, races, and diverse political, economic, and religious ideologies is unattainable and maybe even impossible.

It is perplexing and disturbing.

In our passion to consume and accumulate, we are competitive, confrontational, and self-centered.

Full of fear, insecurity, and greed, we exploit each other and ravage our environment.

We take our pleasures but do not replenish.

We deplete and exhaust the land, abuse our bodies, and violate our spirit.

We create unsustainable imbalances.

We experience and exhibit contradictions that cause confusion and anxiety.

We are capable of infinite compassion and the cruelest brutalities.

We create extraordinary beauty and unimaginable horror.

We are sustained by the fruits of our labor while we destroy the environment from which we derive our bounty.

We celebrate our uniqueness, deny others theirs, and profess our superiority.

We've been graced with abundance, yet many are in great need.

We have been given every freedom, yet to many freedom is denied. Many of us who have every need fulfilled create insatiable wants.

We have every means to resolve our problems, yet they persist.

We exhibit a vengeance for getting ahead but sense we are somehow falling behind in some intangible way.

A Times of London columnist wrote of countries that are "full of people who have all the material comforts they desire, yet lead lives of quiet desperation, understanding nothing but the fact that there is a hole inside of them and that however much food and drink they pour into it, however many cars and television sets they stuff it with . . . it aches."

> "We spend more, but have less; we buy more, but enjoy it less. We have bigger houses and smaller families; more conveniences, but less time; we have more degrees, but less sense; more knowledge, but less judgment; more experts, but more problems; more medicine, but less wellness. We've added years to life, not life to years."
>
> Anonymous

Results of surveys taken in the United States, Western Europe, and Japan to determine the effects of technological progress and the steadily rising standard of living on human health and happiness were essentially the same in all the wealthy industrial nations.

While many believed that knowledge and the state of health had improved, a large majority felt that inner happiness and peace of mind had diminished.

Something is wrong fundamentally.

In stark contrast to our measurable achievements, a quality of life for which we long remains distressingly beyond our reach.

Part II - The Problem

It is the essence, the very nectar of existence that remains stubbornly elusive.

It is a quality of life that can provide us with mental and physical well-being and lead to fewer troubled relationships.

It is the unfulfilled half of our potential of which our higher selves are mindful.

It lies dormant, awaiting release and expression like a genie trapped in a bottle.

World-renowned scientist, humanist, and Pulitzer Prize-winning author Rene Dubos wrote, "Technological societies know how to create material wealth, but their ultimate success will depend on their ability to formulate a postindustrial humanistic culture.

"The shift from obsession with quantitative growth to the search for a better life will not be possible without radical changes in attitudes.

"The Industrial Revolution placed a premium on the kind of intelligence best suited to the invention of manufactured articles, as well as to their production and distribution on a large scale.

"In contrast, a humanistic society would prize more highly skills facilitating better human relationships and more creative interplay between humankind, nature, and technology."

Where once our abundance of natural resources counter-balanced our limited knowledge and vision, today we find ourselves in a new arena.

Now, the limitations of our resources and the extraordinary growth of our population must be compensated for by an expansion of our knowledge and vision.

Similarly, we find that we can no longer engage in our primitive form of conflict resolution, warfare, lest we risk our very existence.

We have neither the resources nor the space to repeat the mistakes of our past.

To do so would be to exhibit an archaic mentality likely to return a few survivors to an archaic time.

Expressing his concern for what he considers to be a central problem of modern civilization, Dubos notes that "science and technology provide us with the means to create almost anything we want, but the development of means without worthwhile goals generates at best a dreary life and may, at worst, lead to tragedy."

A stark example is the discovery of nuclear fission, which was first used to make tens of thousands of thermonuclear warheads.

Today, we stand on the threshold of comprehending the oneness and the interlocking whole of which we are a part.

It informs us that life is not assured; it is dependent upon the interrelationships by which it is sustained.

Because these interrelationships are as fundamental as natural laws, our problems are like those we might suffer by arrogantly defying the law of gravity.

An understanding of the significance of our connectedness and interdependence can serve as a powerful change agent.

It goes to the philosophical heart of our decision-making process.

Attitudes among individuals and institutions must change to recognize the balance in life and the sacredness of mutually beneficial life forms.

We are connected.
Life is fragile.
This understanding is the prerequisite to the next step on our evolutionary journey.

Given the complexity of our world, it is a giant step on an arduous journey.

— *Part II - The Problem* —

Our planet, as of this writing, is divided into some 195 ever-changing sovereign nations with people speaking about 6,500 different languages.

In each nation, a staggering mix of political, economic, cultural, and social factors combine to produce varying qualities of life.

In all these nations, individual, public-sector, and private-sector policies are typically not based on the reality of interdependence.

Decisions, driven by short-term priorities, are commonly based on desires to maximize profit and to retain or gain power, all in the name of progress.

PROFIT, POWER, AND PROGRESS

What can be said of profit, power, and progress in the interrelated and interdependent world in which we exist?

What kind of people are we who allow grotesque disparities to exist between the affluent and the impoverished?

How is it we allow nearly half of our human family to be doomed to a hopeless and unremitting battle for survival, while others of us are over-clothed, over-housed, and so over-fed that we have to go on special diets to lose weight?

This unequal distribution of opportunity and wealth is not accidental.

Fueled by ignorance and its byproduct, greed, it results from economies organized to benefit the insatiable appetites of the opportunistic.

Most individuals and institutions are reluctant to cede self-interest for the common good.

Most countries are unwilling to think beyond sovereignty and national interests.

Instead, shackled with destructive habits and short on vision, they violate relationships with each other and the environment.

In doing so, they court disaster.

This is done in the name of profit, power, and progress.

Consider profit: too often it is the sole motivating force for many who shamelessly sacrifice human decency and environmental protection for short-term personal gains.

We are driven by a surplus of greed and a lack of common sense.

Profit's offspring, exploitive commercialism, fans the fires of materialism.

Enormous sums are invested to convince us that we need to acquire and consume products that are often unnecessary and harmful to us and our environment.

Wealth and status are glorified.
Image supersedes substance.

We plunder and deplete our resources, torture our ailing environment, decimate other species, and pollute our already confused minds.

To what end do we invest ourselves in this fatal frivolity?

Profiteers will always clamor for more and more.
Many achieve enormous wealth.
For each who has much, there are countless others who have precious little.

Rage and fear grow among those who experience economic insecurity.

They are filled with anxiety and despair instead of a sense of community.

Wealth and power, intoxicating and irresistible, blind us to these disparities and their eventual consequences.

Those who exploit innocent others and destroy eco-systems can boast arrogantly of their "achievements," ignorant or in denial of their violations and the eventual consequences of their actions.

It is foolish and irresponsible to maximize profits regardless of human and environmental costs.

Natural resources are not endlessly renewable and self-generating.
People will tolerate only so much exploitation and repression.

— *Part II - The Problem* —

Eventually these violations will lead to famine, economic collapse, and political revolution.

Responsible profit taking is honorable.
Those who are legitimate producers deserve to be rewarded for their considerable risks and efforts.
It is when profit-taking replaces concern for others or for ecosystems that a perversity occurs whereby everyone and everything suffers.

At that point, we are not evolving but devolving.

Those who achieve wealth and power and allow the gap to widen between the rich and the poor promote only inequity, desperation, conflict, ecological ruin, and systemic distress.
Of what value are profit, power, and progress when they violate people, other species, and destroy the conditions that sustain life?

As Aldo Leopold has written, "A thing is right when it tends to preserve the integrity, stability, and beauty of the biotic community.
"It is wrong when it tends otherwise."

The word progress means moving toward a goal.
However, we want to move forward on the right road to the right goal.

While free enterprise requires profit as an incentive to stimulate individual productivity, civilization requires that the welfare of the common good be acknowledged and sustained.
For this, we look to our public sector for the protection of our common interests.

Here too, we find the influence of private interests and the power of money and profits to be pervasive.

Its effect on our democratic form of government is tragic and ominous.

DEMOCRACY

A prominent United States senator said that the influence of money in political campaign financing "… is nothing less than an influence-peddling scheme in which both parties compete to stay in office by selling the country to the highest bidder."

In her book, *The Corruption of American Politics*, veteran Washington journalist Elizabeth Drew wrote, as have so many others, that money is drowning out decency and threatening the underpinnings of democracy itself.

This is obvious and ominous.

Democracy is more than a form of government.
It is a way of life, a formula for just relationships.

The word "democracy" means rule by the people.
Abraham Lincoln described this form of self-government as "government of the people, by the people, for the people," not government of some people, by some people, for some people.

Democracy supports individual freedom and the fundamental dignity and equality of all persons.
Democracy is a form of government in which political power rests with all the people.
Democracy recognizes the intrinsic value of widespread and broad-based input.
Democracy invites the richness of diversity.

Democracy says do not look only to yourself and like-minded people for answers; avail yourself of that which others have to offer, for life is diverse.

Democracy says do not be rigid or inflexible; be open and adaptable, for life is dynamic and ever-changing.

Democracy says do not make participation exclusive; make it inclusive, for life is all encompassing.

Democracy says do not gravitate to extremes; seek moderation, for life requires balance.

Democracy says do not represent only those who have influence; represent all, for life demands justice.

Finally, Democracy says do not tamper with this process, for it is your only hope of survival.

Democracy requires watchdogs.

Always, it is under siege.

This occurs when our capitalistic economic system and our democratic political system clash.

Democracy call for a government of, by, and for the people.

Capitalism calls for profit.

When the quest for and bounty from profits plays a disproportionate role in electing candidates to public office, democracy is vanquished.

When office holders reward their benefactors, there is a gross violation of democracy.

This legal form of institutionalized corruption defeats the spirit of democracy.

When the morality of our government is corrupted, democracy disintegrates.

When the government is controlled by those who seek profit above the welfare of the common good, the democratic process is destroyed.

— Part II - The Problem —

The democratic process represents an appreciation for life, a celebration of diversity, and an acknowledgment of our oneness.

It is a process emanating from our instinct to be free, an irrepressible force.

The ideals of democracy are the ideals of humanity.

For democracy in our public sector and for capitalism in our private sector to work together harmoniously, we must fully understand the implications of our interdependence: the interrelationships of life which sustain both human and ecological systems must be honored.

Democracy is the form of government we have created to protect these interrelationships.

Those who work in the public sector must understand their protective roles.

The common good cannot be sacrificed for the benefit of the powerful.

Those who labor in the free market have similar responsibilities.

The first is to support, not erode, the democratic process.

The second is to profit in ways that do not violate people or our environment.

From these judicious uses of power in both sectors, we all profit and progress.

EDUCATION

An evaluation of our beliefs is always healthy and should be ongoing.
As we mature, our knowledge grows, our beliefs evolve, and our priorities change.
That which is antiquated and dysfunctional must be discarded.
That is normal and healthy.

At one time our planet seemed like an immense and limitless place.
There was true separation between continents and peoples.
Huge territories were undiscovered.
Activities and consequences were confined within definable boundaries.

As we grew and evolved, we moved beyond self-defined limits, reached out, explored, connected, and interacted.
We continued doing this as we became increasingly sophisticated in our abilities to travel, communicate, and trade.

Today, we are a global community.
It is evident that the fate of all living things is interconnected.
We have become responsible for that fate.
We are guardians of life itself.

We live at a pivotal time.
We stand to either learn and benefit from our experiences and knowledge or ignore both and suffer.

It is essential that we embrace a new way of relating.

Whereas the first lesson of evolution was one of conflict, today's is one of kinship.

We need to evolve into something more than we've been.

We are called upon to make a crucial decision and choose either a world divided against itself—engaged in power struggles between its parts—or one whose richly diverse elements work together for their mutual benefit.

The choice is obvious.

It is important that we focus on our common interests rather than on stubborn positions that lead only to conflict.

Once our interests are defined, options for mutual gain can be explored and developed.

We can then address the issues that benefit everyone rather than cling to political or religious ideologies that separate us.

If we hope to transcend our divisiveness, our attention must be directed at the interdependence of diverse interests.

More than the outcome of any debate, we need to protect this kind of approach and process.

Until we do, we are ill-fated.

We no longer have the luxury of ignorance or greed.

We now exist in a world community where problems anywhere have the potential to affect anyone anywhere.

Ultimately, the problems of cities and the environment, of production and consumption, and of crime, health, and world peace are educational problems.

Our task, for which our age is well suited, is education.

However, nearly a billion people entered the 21st century unable to read a book or sign their names.

— *Part II - The Problem* —

Less than one per cent of what the world spent every year on weapons was needed to put every child into school by the year 2,000 and yet it didn't happen.

This must change.

An educated and enlightened public will move from alienation to community, from despair to hope, from idleness to action, from ignorance to knowledge, and from apathy to empathy.

People will return to the political process.
As they do, politics will return to the people.

Ecological balance will be integrated with human productivity, social welfare will be tempered by individual responsibility, and localism and globalism will share equal importance.

RELIGION

Is there a need for a "religion," i.e., a belief system, in all of this? The answer is that we require a set of beliefs grounded in reality and void of anything supernatural to guide us as we navigate through life.

More specifically, we need a vision relevant to the complex and increasingly sophisticated age in which we live, a vision that defines what is sacred here and now in this life, not "out there" somewhere in some afterlife.

We need a definition and related ethic so clear and universal that it changes forever our understanding of profit, power, and progress.

We need a vision, a basis for morality, that enlightens the worlds of commerce, politics, and religion itself.

Such a belief system would play a central role in our lives.

It would expand knowledge and justice and reduce ignorance and suffering.

It would embody inclusiveness in the broadest sense.

It would diffuse historical rivalries and contemporary adversaries engaged in ruinous relationships.

It would draw us together.

It would change the way we care for each other, our environment, and ourselves.

It would do what most of us want a belief system to do.

It would help us achieve a healthier, more peaceful, and just world.

We exist at the threshold of a new way to understand and live life.

We have evolved through the agrarian and industrial ages to a post-industrial, high-tech digital information and communication age.

For the first time, we have instantaneous, global communication.

We are poised to disseminate the information necessary to develop a new world view: a humanistic culture where the outlook is for the long term; where integrative approaches to problem solving are utilized; where poverty is eradicated; and where wasteful consumption patterns are eliminated.

Our limitation is not technology, it is old-world thinking and ethics among leaders and followers who, with a limited understanding of our reality, have vested and narrow interests in maintaining the status quo.

Much of our inability to advance stems from failure to discuss long-term interests, from unnecessary polarization, and from excessive divisions along ideological lines.

In a world that abounds with astonishing diversity, one wonders how we can subscribe to the rigidity that is at the core of our problems.

Our planet is small.

We are not isolated from or unaffected by our neighbors as we were in our past.

We are now required to satisfy ourselves as individuals and as members of larger communities.

We are like a body of people involved in a grand experiment that might be described in the following manner.

Imagine a beautiful island resplendent with majestic mountains, lush valleys, gorgeous beaches, clean air, sparkling waters, and extraordinary varieties of plants and animals.

As an experiment, a remarkably diverse group of people are loaded onto a boat and sent to live on this island.

— Part II - The Problem —

These people possess every conceivable talent and skill to create very comfortable lives for themselves.

Three things are asked of these people: take care of your health; work together in harmony; replenish what you consume.

For satisfying these three simple requirements, these people are guaranteed lives of peace and abundance.

Like this theoretical experiment, humanity had the same opportunity.

Through history, the combination of our natural resources and our human skills and abilities offered us extraordinary opportunities that we were not yet wise enough to recognize.

Instead, we became embroiled in power struggles over our different ethnicities, territories, and belief systems.

We chose to address our differences—ones that presented unlimited opportunities—as opposing principles in competition rather than as complementary ones that enhance each other.

Self-centered tribes, regions, and nations alienated and made enemies of each other.

No one worked for the common good.

This transformed our elegant potential into countless and ongoing tragedies.

We have each become like tiny islands with limited resources.

We defend, rather than share, our unique qualities.

As a consequence, few find contentment.

It never seems to occur to us that our many needs are mutual and connected.

Most of us are unable to comprehend the intrinsic value and infinite potential of our diversity and differences.

PRIMITIVE BELIEFS

Countless primitive beliefs and belief systems emerged on different parts of our planet at different times through our ancient history.

We call them religions.

We have had and continue to have many religions.

The effect of these unique creeds has not been to bring us together but to separate us permanently.

Often, they begin as cults.

As each belief system grows, it gains power and inclusiveness.

At the core of each is typically a creation story, often a variation of an earlier story.

Mystery and supernatural events such as divine revelation—communication with a deity or other supernatural entity—and miracles are central to each belief system.

Each religion has its sacred places and rituals.

All of it is contrived out of ideas that were popular at a particular time or built upon the evolution of former ideas.

Stories grew from fiction to fact, developed into "religions" and declared themselves to be "sacred."

This development was precisely backwards.

Only out of an understanding first of what is truly sacred, in a nonreligious and universal sense, can a belief system emerge.

Given the origins of religions it is not surprising that there is fierce competition between them that often results in horrendous bloodshed.

Fortunately, with the passage of time, the credibility of these belief systems has come under ever-greater scrutiny.

The complexity of our time and magnitude of the problems that we face raise profound questions for ancient religions.

Quickly growing and increasingly integrated populations further complicate our lives and compound our problems.

Many people have begun to question these old religious belief systems and even the idea of religion.

What is religion and what is its mission?

Is it to dwell on, venerate, and interpret the past?

Or is it to develop new beliefs based on current knowledge?

Ones that will nurture and sustain us as we confront each other and the new realities in our increasingly interconnected and interdependent world?

How can religions, so divided themselves, accomplish such tasks?

Enlightened by the collective wisdom of our past, many of us are coming to realize that in order to survive, we must shed the superstitious religions that hinder our progress and find a universal belief system that can unite the world's communities.

It seems that the role of many theologians is to forever study ancient texts and endlessly debate their interpretations.

Most theologians are swept away by, absorbed in, and dependent upon the existing current of religious institutional inertia.

Many are buffered by academic insulation.

It is unlikely that many theologians would be bold enough, could risk, or would even want to introduce the new thinking that is needed.

Somewhat of a counter movement, The Clergy Project, has begun and is growing rapidly.

It is an online community for active and former clergy who no longer hold supernatural beliefs.

Part II - The Problem

It is a "safe house" where members freely discuss the challenges they face in leaving ministry and establishing a new life.

There are further stubborn questions for our ailing religious institutions.

How can religion end the frenzy of self-centeredness that everywhere afflicts individuals, groups, and nations?

How can religion convince the powerful who have vested interests in the status quo that their attitudes and actions are not only unsustainable but also catastrophic and terminal to themselves and everyone else?

How can religion diffuse fixed historical rivalries and debilitating and ruinous conflicts among countless contemporary adversaries?

Since people rarely act until there is a crisis, how can religions prepare their faithful for impending disasters that could be overwhelming?

At this time, we are not lacking in religious institutions that could address these issues.

High priests and priestesses are not in short supply.

There is quite a varied menu of teachers and scriptures from which to choose.

It is remarkable that so many of these religions claim exclusive possession of "divinely inspired and infallible truth."

Even more remarkable is the unwillingness or inability of so many people to question these claims.

Many people are content to embrace a particular myth, adopt a creed, or fall under the spell of a charismatic personality.

Some followers are prepared to do almost anything, including sacrificing their lives to satisfy the doctrines of their faith.

Tragically, in the name of fervently held religious beliefs, some of these followers become fanatics and take the lives of fellow humans.

It seems never to occur to them that what they do is more important than what they believe.

Most of this behavior is rooted in ignorance.

Because we have a need to ease our miseries, calm our fears, band together to compete with other groups, and generally understand the cause and purpose of life, we are receptive to ideas that satisfy these needs.

As a consequence, we are overwhelmed with opposing dogma and rituals as religions compete for followers, financial support, and power.

The path that should have led to clarity instead has led to other cells in the religious prison block.

Needless complexities, theatrics, and exploitation among multiple religions, sects, schools, creeds, and cults have distorted reality.

We praise distant mythological deities as we exploit our neighbors.

We dream of the "hereafter" as we destroy the "here."

Convinced that we are the exceptions that will be saved in an afterlife, we ignore our responsibility for saving ourselves in this life.

We are willing, even anxious, to take giant leaps of faith, but refuse to take even small steps toward sound reason and common sense.

We elevate fictional stories of gods and creation, fabricated by ourselves, to the status of divinely inspired dogma, freeze them in texts, and upon these shaky foundations build and perpetuate religious institutions.

Many people have begun to see this nonsense for what it is.

Doctrines that were formed before the age of science and written by churchmen profoundly ignorant of their world no longer hold any appeal for growing numbers of better-informed individuals.

Mainline churches have begun to lose millions of members.

Still, these antiquated religions live on perpetuated by enormous institutional inertia.

— *Part II - The Problem* —

Swept away in this tidal wave, theologians and clergy are forever engaged in a litany of interpretation upon interpretation of word after word of ancient stories that were written creatively in the first place.

When they are not involved in the interpretation of ancient texts, they are involved in interpreting each other's interpretations.

Interpretation, known as exegesis, has become an industry unto itself.

As a consequence, fundamental and uncomplicated messages about proper human conduct and just human relationships have gotten muddled, diluted, and rendered impotent.

Religions have fragmented into multiple forms of expression.

Those who have longed for clarity and direction have gotten increasingly alienated and confused.

Brutal behavior, social violence, and environmental degradation continue to worsen.

There exists no belief system to draw humanity together to eliminate its problems.

A glaring irony is that our religious divisions account for a large share of our armed conflict.

Through the years, many bloody wars, genocide, crusades, missionary atrocities, and persecutions have taken place in the name of religion.

Intelligent people find these occurrences and their religious justifications to be reprehensible.

Many otherwise intelligent people are reluctant to engage in open conversations on religion, as religious beliefs—life-long habits and coveted addictions—are very personal and highly charged.

Believers find it impossible to remain dispassionate and rational.

When the beliefs of religious adherents are challenged, even politely, responses are often emotional, defensive, and even violent.

We are cautioned not to speak about religion.

It is a shunned subject that ignites easily.

There is something very wrong with all of this that screams for a remedy.

PART III
THE SOLUTION

"No matter how exalted we think ourselves, all that we can know and become has a material basis obedient to the decipherable laws of physics and chemistry.

"And no matter how intellectually far above the remainder of life we lift ourselves, and however technically proficient we become, we will stay a biological species, biological in origin, and thence adapted in mind and body to the living world that cradled us."
—Edward O. Wilson, 1998 Phi Beta Kappa Oration
Harvard University

CONTEXT, PERSPECTIVE, AND TIME FRAMES

A favorite quote of mine is from a person named Rahel: "If you wish to astonish the whole world, tell the simple truth."
His statement begs the question.
What *is* the simple truth?
The simple truth about what?

In my context, it is the simple truth about life.
What makes life healthy?
What sustains life?
What in life is "sacred"?

Most people associate the word "sacred" with religion.
As noted earlier, sacred also has a nonreligious meaning that is grounded in reality and goes to the essence of life itself.
That meaning of sacred is *that in life which at our peril we cannot violate, damage, dishonor, or destroy.*

There is a phenomenon that I refer to as *the way of life*, which is in complete alignment with the nonreligious understanding of sacred.
If we honor the way of life, we prosper.
If we violate it, we suffer needlessly.

To explore, discover, and understand the way of life requires context, perspective, and time frames.
For these, we will turn to three areas.

First, we will review some of what we know from cosmology, the origin and structure of the universe.

Second, we turn to evolutionary biology.
How long has this planet and life been here?
How long have we been here?
What has life been through to get this far?

Third, we look at the world of religion.
From where have all these religions come and why?

Danish philosopher and theologian Soren Kierkegaard observed that "Searching for truth is like searching in a pitch-dark room for a black cat that isn't there."

Truth is elusive.
But truth and elements of truth are discoverable.
Truth is stubborn, tough, and patient.
These things we call facts are stubborn things.

Chief Justice Oliver Wendell Holmes observed that "Truth is tough. It will not break, like a bubble, at a touch; you may kick it around all day like a football, and it will be round and full at evening."

COSMOLOGY

From cosmology, we know that every hour we travel in excess of a billion miles!
How do we do that?

It is as though we are on a spacecraft within a spacecraft within another spacecraft, at least.

The first spacecraft on which we are passengers is our planet as it orbits the star that we call the Sun at a speed of 65,000 miles an hour.

Our solar system is the second spacecraft.

We are passengers on it as it orbits our galaxy, the Milky Way, at 600,000 miles per hour.

The Milky Way, the third spacecraft on which we travel, is speeding along among other galaxies with the expansion of the universe in excess of a billion miles per hour.

This gives us a total well in excess of a billion miles that we travel *every hour* of our lives.

For all we know, we may be, as some scientists believe, on a fourth spacecraft, our universe, as it travels among other universes in a multiverse.

Our planet, Earth, is small, only 7,926 miles in diameter and 24,000 miles in circumference.

In volume, it is only 3 millionths the size of the Sun.

We exist in a solar system comprised of the Sun, eight planets, the Kuiper Belt (a region with a collection of bodies beyond the eight planets), 183 moons (Earth: 1, Mars: 2, Jupiter: 67, Saturn: 62, Uranus:

27, Neptune: 13, and in the Kuiper Belt: Pluto – smaller than our moon – with 5 moons and other dwarf planets with 5 moons) with more being discovered all of the time; millions of asteroids; and countless comets and meteoroids.

Of the eight planets, four are known as the inner and terrestrial planets: Mercury (3,029 miles diameter), Venus (7,519 miles diameter), Earth (7,926 miles diameter), and Mars (4,223 miles diameter).

The four outer planets are known as the gas giants.
They are comprised mostly of hydrogen and helium gas with relatively small rocky cores.
These outer planets, that represent 99 percent of the mass of all the planets, are Jupiter (89,000 miles diameter), Saturn (75,000 miles diameter), Uranus (32,000 miles diameter), and Neptune (31,000 miles diameter).

The Sun, in comparison, is so large (865,000 miles diameter) that it comprises 99.85% of the total mass of our solar system.

As our planet orbits the Sun at 65,000 miles per hour, simultaneously, it rotates on its axis at 1,000 miles an hour.
To rotate fully, it takes what we call a day.

As we orbit the Sun, our moon, 238,857 miles away, orbits us every 27 days, 7 hours, and 43 minutes.

Earth is about 93 million miles from the Sun.
The closest planet to the Sun, Mercury, a very hot planet, is 36 million miles from the sun.
Venus, 67.2 million miles from the sun, is hotter than Mercury.
The reason is that Venus has a very thick heat-trapping atmosphere whereas Mercury, with no atmosphere, radiates its heat back out to space.

— *Part III - The Solution* —

To give you a sense of the size of our solar system, Pluto, in the Kuiper Belt, is about 3,666,000,000 miles from the Sun.

The circuit that Earth orbits around the Sun is 600 million miles. To orbit once, it takes what we call a year.

While all this is going on, our solar system orbits the Milky Way galaxy.
The Milky Way name comes from its appearance as a dim "milky" glowing band arching across the night sky, in which the naked eye cannot distinguish individual stars.

Envision our solar system: The Sun (comprised of exploding gases: 75% hydrogen, 24% helium, and 1% other gases) and its eight planets (four solid and four comprised mostly of gas), 183 moons, millions of asteroids, meteoroids, comets, and the objects in the Kuiper Belt, all orbit the Milky Way galaxy at 600,000 miles per hour like a huge self-contained space station more than seven billion miles in diameter.
How long does it take for our solar system to orbit the Milky Way galaxy one time?
Recall that it takes Earth a year to orbit the Sun at 65,000 miles an hour.
In contrast, our solar system orbits the galaxy at 600,000 miles per hour.
But even at that speed it takes *225 million years* for our solar system to orbit the Milky Way galaxy one time.

The Milky Way Galaxy contains 200-400 billion stars.
When we look into the sky on a very clear and starry night, we can see about 2,500 stars.
That's about one hundred-millionth of the stars in the Milky Way galaxy!

Astronomers estimate that there are 100 billion habitable Earth-like planets in the Milky Way and 50 sextillion ones in the universe!

The nearest star to us is Proxima Centauri.

It is one of a three-star system that includes Alpha and Beta Centauri, which tumble over each other while Proxima Centauri orbits them.

To reach Proxima Centauri from our solar system, traveling at the speed of light, 186,000 miles per second—a speed at which we could fly around Earth seven times in one second—requires four years and three months.

That's to reach the nearest star of approximately 200-400 billion in our galaxy!

Just how big is our galaxy?

The Milky Way is 100,000 light-years wide.

A light-year is the distance covered in a year traveling at the speed of light, 186,000 miles per second: 5,880 billion miles, nearly six trillion miles.

Multiply that times 100,000 and you have the distance across our galaxy.

There is another way, perhaps a little more comprehensible, to visualize something 100,000 light-years wide.

If we started at one side of our galaxy and traveled across it at 186,000 miles a second for every second of every minute of every hour of every day of every week of every month of every year for 100,000 years, we would reach the other side.

As recently as the 1920s, we thought the Milky Way galaxy was the entire universe.

That was an error equivalent to thinking that Earth is flat.

As large as our galaxy is, we know it is only one of hundreds of billions of large galaxies in the observable universe.

The observable universe consists of the galaxies and other matter that we can in principle observe from Earth because light or other signals from those objects is visible and has had time to reach us since the beginning of the cosmological expansion.

Part III - The Solution

It is referred to as the observable universe because our vision is obscured by dust, gases, and billions of stars.

It is estimated that there are trillions of galaxies and dwarf galaxies in the universe.

A dwarf galaxy may have *only* several billion stars while a typical galaxy has hundreds of billions of stars.

The nearest large galaxy is Andromeda which contains about a *trillion stars.*

To get a sense of the unimaginable and incomprehensible size of the universe, consider that to reach the Andromeda galaxy from our galaxy, the Milky Way, we would have to travel at the speed of light, 186,000 miles per second, for *2,500,000 years.*

That's just to reach the nearest galaxy of trillions of galaxies!

Galaxies are organized into clusters and super clusters.

The Milky Way, Andromeda, and more than thirty other galaxies exist in a cluster by the name of the Local Group.

The Local Group is 10 million light-years wide.

We would have to travel 186,000 miles a second for 10 million years to cross it!

The Local Group sits on the edge of a super cluster by the name of Virgo.

Virgo is hundreds of millions of light-years wide.

To cross it requires hundreds of millions of years of travel at 186,000 miles per second.

It contains thousands of galaxies.

Galaxies, like our own Milky Way, are carried along by the expansion of the Universe and will move apart from every other galaxy unless they're close enough to hold together with gravity.

Most of the galaxies in the Universe, because of the Big Bang and the consequent continual expansion of the Universe, are moving away from us at speeds in excess of a billion miles per hour.

The galaxies themselves aren't moving very quickly through space, it's the space itself which is expanding, and the galaxies are being carried along with it.

Space—the universe—is expanding faster than the speed of light!

To envision this, imagine the universe as a loaf of raisin bread baking in the oven.

The rising dough is the universe expanding.

The raisins (galaxies) move with the rising dough.

Note that the raisins (galaxies) move away from other raisins (galaxies) as the bread (the universe) rises and expands.

Scientists are now pondering the probability that there are many more universes.

Let's review all of this briefly.

In general terms, our universe consists of clusters and super clusters of galaxies.

These galaxies contain billions of stars like our Sun.

Planets orbit some of these stars.

Moons orbit some of these planets.

We exist on a planet, Earth, orbited by a moon.

Our planet and its moon orbit a star, our Sun, at 65,000 miles per hour.

The Sun, along with the rest of the bodies in our solar system, orbits the Milky Way galaxy at 600,000 miles per hour.

The Milky Way galaxy, with all its solar systems (stars, planets, moons, etc.) travels outward among other galaxies with the expansion of the universe at speeds in excess of a billion miles an hour—*faster than the speed of light.*

This is the incredible system in which we exist and of which our planet is an extremely tiny fragment, a mere speck on the blueprint of existence.

EARTH

Let's return to planet Earth and consider how long our planet has been here, when life first appeared, and when we humans arrived.

To do that, we turn to radiometric dating and the fossil record.

From radiometric dating, the rate of radioactive decay is constant over time, we know Earth has existed for about 4.56 billion years.

Our galaxy has existed for 13.2 billion years in a universe 13.8 billion years old.

According to the fossil record, which is a trace of an organism of a past geologic age, life in the form of primitive single-cell microorganisms or microbes, too small to be seen by the human eye, began on Earth about 3.8 billion years ago.

For nearly a billion years, Earth had no life.

It took more than another 3 billion years before the first multicellular plants and animals appeared.

That was about 670 million years ago.

About 525 million years ago in the Paleozoic Era, the Age of Vertebrates and Invertebrates began.

After hundreds of millions of years, this age yielded insects and the beginning of fish and reptiles.

About 245 million years ago in the Mesozoic Era, the Age of Reptiles began.

This was the time the dinosaurs lived and ruled.

It lasted for about 180 million years.

The Age of Reptiles ended about 65 million years ago when an asteroid, estimated to be 7 to 50 miles in diameter, struck Earth in an area now known as Chicxulub, Mexico in the Yucatan Peninsula.

The energy released by the Chicxulub impact was beyond a billion times the power of the atomic bomb dropped on Hiroshima.

The impact triggered earthquakes, tsunamis, and an explosion of debris that blanketed the Earth in layers of dust and sediment.

It wiped out large dinosaurs and giant marine reptiles and ended the Age of the Reptiles.

About 65 million years ago began the Cenozoic Era sometimes called the Age of the Mammals although some mammals first appeared more than 200 million years ago.

Mammals are a hairy species that feed their young from mammary glands.

Mammals range in size from shrews that weigh 1/14 ounce (2 grams) to whales that weigh 140 tons (127,000 kg).

The Age of Mammals is the age in which we live.
We are one of about 5,500 species of mammals.

Something very significant, the beginning of nurturing behavior, occurred with the arrival of mammals.

In mammals, we see the beginning of the shift from the reptilian brain to the more advanced brain.

Reptiles hatch from eggs.
Although some reptiles tend their nest, most reptiles do not take care of their eggs.

Young reptiles are able to feed and care for themselves.

By contrast, mammals nurture their young.
Great emphasis is placed on feeding, protecting, and teaching skills to the young in order for them to survive on their own.

— *Part III - The Solution* —

Moreover, mammals possess the most highly developed brain of all animals.

A large brain-size in relation to their body and the brain structure known as the cerebral cortex provide mammals with highly developed intelligence and senses that increase their ability to learn and perform detailed tasks.

What about us?
How long have modern humans been here?

It is thought that about five to six million years ago the succession of species that gave rise to us separated from the succession that led to the apes.

From a common ancestor, the apes moved off in one direction and we, the hominids or family of humans, moved off in another.

The first genus of the hominids, five to six million years ago, was Sahelandthropus tachadensis, the remains of which were discovered in Chad, Africa in 2002.

It was followed by genuses Orrorin tugenensis, Ardipithecus, Australopithecus, Kenyanthropus, Paranthropus and finally our genus, Homo, showed up about 2.3 million years ago.

These Homo genus beings were not Homo sapiens, however, but Homo habilis, the earliest known member of our genus.

These were not what we consider to be modern humans.

In between the emergence of Homo habilis and the eventual arrival of Homo sapiens sapiens (us), were numerous Homo species (such as homo rudolfensis, homo ergaster, homo erectus, homo antecessor, homo heidelbergensis, homo neanderthalensis, and more).

In 2004 on the island of Flores in Indonesia, the remains of a homo species were discovered that was about three-feet six-inches tall, weighing about 55 pounds.

Extinct now for at least 50,000 years, it is thought to be the only homo species that may have co-existed with us.

It was named homo floresiensis, nicknamed "the Hobbit," after the tiny folk in J.R.R. Tolkien's book of the same name.

It was in Africa, about 300,000 years ago, that modern humans, homo sapiens (sensible humans), emerged.
From there, we spread through Africa, into Asia and Europe, and to the rest of our world.

The family of humans began five to six million years ago as hunter-gatherers and remained so—through all the genuses and homo species—until about 10,000 to 12,000 years ago.
At that time, with the domestication of plants and animals in various locations, our Agrarian Age began.

We remained in the Agrarian Age until the late 1700s, when the Industrial Revolution began in England.

By the mid-1800s, the Industrial Revolution spread to Belgium, Germany, France, and the United States.
Eventually, it spread to all the industrial nations.
By the middle of the 1900s, we began to transition into a post-industrial high-technology age.

This led directly to the Information and Communication Age that emerged in the latter part of the 20th century.
For the first time in our history, we were able to disseminate information almost anywhere instantly.
The Information Age has allowed rapid global communications and networking to shape modern society.

Our computing capabilities are growing exponentially.
It is likely that change will continue at an unprecedented rate, gaining momentum with time.
Everything, everywhere, will be connected.
We will be able to know anything, anytime, anywhere.

— *Part III - The Solution* —

Through the years, our population has continued to grow. The following is a glimpse at how our population has risen.

Year	Population
1 AD	200 million
1000	275 million
1500	450 million
1650	500 million
1750	750 million
1804	1 billion
1900	1.6 billion
1927	2 billion
1960	3 billion
1975	4 billion
1987	5 billion
1999	6 billion
2011	7 billion
2030	8.5 billion (United Nations' projection)
2050	9.7 billion (United Nations' projection)
2100	11.2 billion (United Nations' projection)

It took from the very beginning of the evolution of our species, about 300,000 years ago, to the year 1900 for us to reach a population of 1.6 billion.

Then something extraordinary happened.

It's something that will likely never again occur on this planet.

From the year 1900 to 1960, our population jumped from 1.6 billion people to 3 billion.

In sixty years, we nearly doubled the population that it took all of evolution to produce.

Then, in the next *thirty-nine years,* we added an astonishing 3 billion people to reach a population of 6 billion in 1999.

In other words, from 1960 to 1999, 39 years, we added as many people, 3 billion, as it took for our entire previous existence, 300,000 years, to accumulate.

United Nations' projections are that we will reach 8.5 billion in 2030.

It is estimated that in 2050 our population will be 9.7 billion.

The latest United Nations' projections are that world population will nearly stabilize at just above 11 billion persons after 2100.

At our current rate of growth, we add about 75 million people a year—*nearly a million and a half a week*—to our global population.

If we take a survey of the social and political attitudes, beliefs, and behaviors of a representative sample of our population, do a statistical distribution with our data and plot the results on a graph, we typically come up with a classic bell-shaped curve also known as a normal distribution.

The area at the top in the center of the curve is known as the normal range of behavior, average behavior.

It is here where we find common ground and agreement.

Off to the right and left of the curve are standard deviations from the normal range.

Beyond these standard deviations are extreme deviations from the normal range.

What does all of this mean?

It means that whatever the issue may be, the people on one side of the curve will have very different views than those on the opposite side.

This results in opposition, conflict, and strife, up to and including wars, all of which are common in our world.

This very normal and predictable bell-shaped curve, a snapshot of humanity, is a remarkable phenomenon.

This very predictable pattern contributes to and practically guarantees life's multiple interpersonal problems, challenges, unpredictability, instability, and uncertainty.

This bell-shaped curve presents humanity with its greatest challenge: how to bridge our differences, the products of evolution.

We make it worse politically when we tamper with this normal distribution.

— *Part III - The Solution* —

We do that by a process known as Gerrymandering, rigging and radicalizing voting districts, that attempts to establish a political advantage for a particular party.

Gerrymandering guarantees that there will not be a normal distribution that results in normal constructive opposition.
Instead, we end up with hyperpolarization that radicalizes opposition political parties rendering them unable to work together for the common good.

Further contributing to life's unpredictability, instability, and uncertainty is the fickleness of nature.
Natural disasters include earthquakes, hurricanes (also known as typhoons and cyclones), volcanoes, tornadoes, tsunamis, forest fires, floods, droughts, and other severe weather phenomena.
Also contributing are a vast number of illnesses that we contract and from which we suffer, and an extraordinary array of accidents that occur regularly.
In addition, because we have so many people and are a young species that has been largely ignorant of the physical reality and the behavioral demands of the reality in which we live, and which enables us to exist, we have created an interrelated web of life-threatening environmental problems.

We are depleting our resources: forests, fisheries, range lands, croplands, and plant and animal species.

We are destroying the biological diversity on which evolution thrives.
This is called the sixth great wave of extinction in the history of life on earth, different from the others in that it is caused not by an external event like an asteroid impact or climate change (which caused all but one of the extinctions) but by us, humanity.

With powerful new electrical and diesel pumping techniques, we are draining our aquifers and lowering our water tables.

We are systemically polluting our air, water, and soil, and consequently our food chain.

We are depleting the stratospheric ozone that shields us from harmful ultraviolet radiation.

And, we are experiencing symptoms of global warming and climate change: heat waves, devastating droughts, destruction of crop- lands, dying forests, accelerated species extinction, dying coral reefs, melting glaciers, rising sea levels, more frequent and intense storms, coastal flooding, more rapid spread of diseases, poisoned oceans (acidification), famine and starvation, human migration, heat deaths, economic collapse, and social conflict and war.

Despite enormous scientific evidence and consensus on climate change and global warming, many people, for a variety of "reasons," deny and dismiss the rate and extent of global warming, its significance, or its connection to human behavior.

> The environmental problems just noted are by no means exhaustive.
> There are additional serious environmental problems.
> Environmental problems are not isolated from each other.
> The synergistic interplay of these problems results in more problems.
> The implications and consequences are unpredictable and ominous

This thing we call life, perilous and far from certain, is a fragile phenomenon.

It is up and down like a seesaw on which we are sitting.

In our theatres, where we have for thousands of years told the stories of our lives, we have for symbols the classic masks of comedy and tragedy to represent joy and sorrow.

Life has always been this way.

SCIENCE AND RELIGION

To explain life, for answers, we have turned to two disciplines that are opposed diametrically, science and religion.

Science is very formal and rigid in the determination of its principles and theories.

A scientific theory must survive a regimen of objective testing and re-testing by any observers and testers at any place and produce identical results time after time before it is accepted as fact.

Science is almost perverse in its methodology of testing in attempts to get its theories to break.

Science is a very open process that welcomes and celebrates change when new discoveries are made.

Religion, on the other hand, is an untested collection of dogmatic principles.

It is derived typically from supernatural sources and that which is referred to as "divine revelation," meaning communication with gods and other supernatural entities.

Religion is a phenomenon that was born when "priests" and "priestesses" invented themselves, which they continue to do today.

Unlike science, religion need not concern itself with objective reality.

Verification is dependent upon faith.

Religion does not like challenges or changes to its dogma.

The alteration of a few words of so-called "revealed religion" can unravel and splinter religions into smaller groups.

These in turn unravel and splinter into even smaller groups.

Christianity, for example, the religion in which I was raised, we know from the *World Christian Encyclopedia*, has approximately thirty-three thousand sects and denominations.

Evidence of religion, art, and recorded events dates back thirty to forty thousand years.

There have been an estimated one hundred thousand religions.

From the aforementioned survey, we know there exists about ten thousand religions today.

One hundred and fifty of these have a million or more followers.

Some of the better-known religions include Hinduism, which originated six thousand years ago; Judaism, four thousand years ago; Buddhism, Confucianism, and Taoism, twenty-six hundred years ago; Christianity, two thousand years ago; and Islam, fourteen hundred years ago.

We've worshipped everything from the sun, to the moon, to Egyptian pharaohs and Roman emperors.

Then, we created mythological gods in our own image.

Throughout history, we've worshipped many gods of countless polytheistic religions, meaning religions with multiple gods.

About four thousand years ago, in the Middle East, someone came up with the idea that there is just one god.

Keep in mind that this was just someone's idea.

Someone like you or me.

This idea marked the beginning of the western concept of what we refer to as monotheism, one god.

The religion that first practiced monotheism was Judaism.

The god was Yahweh, misspelled Jehovah in the King James Version of the Bible.

— *Part III - The Solution* —

About fourteen hundred years later, 2,600 years ago, Buddhism in India, and Confucianism and Taoism in China, emerged as powerful religious movements in the East.

These are belief systems with no gods.

In the last forty years of the first century A.D., in the approximate years 60 to 100, no one knows for sure, and long after the events that were claimed to have occurred, the New Testament gospels Mark,

Matthew, Luke, and John were written decades apart.

Who wrote these stories?

People theorize about the authors, but no one knows who wrote these gospels.

They were written anonymously by early Church teachers.

Later, to bestow legitimacy, the authorships were assigned to four evangelistic saints, Mark, Matthew, Luke, and John.

What were these gospel writers doing?

Theologians agree that each of the writers had their own agenda and bias.

What were they doing?

As Albert Einstein observed, we can't solve our problems from the same level of thinking from which they originated.

These writers were trying to go to the next level of thinking.

The Jewish laws had been around for hundreds of years.

It was time to move on, advance, and evolve.

The writers were radical, progressive, and inclusive.

They reached out to the gentiles.

They sought to help the poor.

Their followers congregated in homes.

Congregations formed (churches).

Theologians agree that the gospel authors created stories to match the prophecy of the Old Testament written hundreds of years earlier.

To embellish their stories, the writers employed the practice, common at the time, of incorporating fictional elements drawn from ancient writings, circulating for centuries, of heroes and gods from pagan, generally rural and polytheistic, religions.

Today, we call this practice plagiarism.

In particular, they "borrowed" heavily from a rival and major religion in the Roman Empire, Mithraism, which had existed for hundreds of years.

It originated in Persia, which is now Iran.

Mithraism, based on a fictional character named Mithra, was popular in the first century with Roman soldiers and civil servants and was a main competitor to Christianity for the first four centuries.

The storyline of Mithraism, not surprisingly, was strikingly similar to Christianity.

A kind of formula for these types of stories existed back then.

Because there was no such thing as plagiarism, one used what one liked from earlier stories.

So, as the story goes, Mithra was born of a virgin. At his birth were adoring shepherds and magi kings.

Kings were inserted into these stories commonly to represent royalty, to signify that the birth was important.

Mithra's birth, like numerous other supernatural heroes and gods, was celebrated on December 25, the same day the Christians adopted.

What's so special about December 25 as the date is used in numerous stories?

It's four days after the winter solstice, December 21, when in the Northern hemisphere the sun is at its lowest point.

— *Part III - The Solution* —

By December 25, it was evident to the ancients that the sun was rising again.

It was a time for celebration and an auspicious day to be born as the sun, worshipped as a god, was rising.

The rising sun provided the idea for ascension.

In the tale of Mithra were stories of miracles, resurrection, and ascension.

Mithra, considered the Way, the Truth and the Light, was revered as the Good Shepherd, the Savior and the Messiah.

The similarity in story lines made possible the easy conversion of Mithraism's followers to Christianity.

Out of all of this, a new story was created, which most learned theologians agree is fictitious, and a new religion born, Christianity.

With it came another god, Christ, from the Greek word Christos, an interpretation of the Hebrew word for messiah, mashiach, meaning the anointed one as prophesied in the Old Testament.

At some point, somewhere, someone declared that these contrived and plagiarized stories were the divinely inspired and infallible words of God.

In other words, people were led to believe that the same God that they created in their stories was responsible for the stories they created.

It is not surprising that many scholars and countless and growing numbers of people have concluded that the story is fiction and that Jesus is a fictional character created by the early Christian community.

These scholars base their arguments on several key points:

1. There is no mention of a miracle-working Jesus in 1st century secular (non-religious) sources. While there were reputable historians at that time, no one recorded these remarkable events that were supposed to have taken place.

2. The epistles, written earlier than the gospels, provide no evidence of a recent historical Jesus.

3. The Jesus narrative is paralleled in earlier Middle Eastern myths about dying and rising gods like Baal, Osiris, Attis, Adonis and Dumuzi/Tammuz, all of which survived into the Hellenistic and Roman periods and influenced early Christianity.

About fourteen hundred years ago in Mecca, the leading city of Arabia, another prophet, Mohammed (570-633), appeared.
He, too, heard the inerrant and infallible words of God.

As Mohammed was illiterate and could not read or write, he had a scribe make notes of what he heard.
These notes, recorded in small segments over a twenty-three-year period, were compiled in a book known as the Koran (Qur'an).
Four-fifths the length of the New Testament, the Koran is considered by Muslims to be the final and infallible revelation of God's will.

Born was another religion, Islam, meaning peace and surrender or submission to God.
And, we got another god, Allah, meaning literally "The God."
The one true God.

We have given gods great powers.
We say they are omnipotent, meaning that they are all-powerful; omnipresent, meaning that they exist everywhere; and omniscient, meaning that they have all learning and knowledge.

These stories, and the religions and belief systems formed out of and around them, have caused great worldwide confusion, conflict, suffering, and wars.
Many wars, as noted below, have been fought over these stories.
We kill each other over these stories.

— Part III - The Solution —

It is the ultimate irony and a complete absurdity that we create these stories to establish examples of exemplary behavior and proper rules for living, then we kill each other over these stories.

One does not have to be a genius to conclude that there is something absurd and fundamentally wrong here.

Billions of people live in ignorance and/or denial of religion's absurdities.

What has the dark side of religion wrought?

Consider the following examples, excerpted and, in some instances, paraphrased from Michael Shermer, author of The *Moral Arc* and numerous other books.

Religious Extremism. Religion has led some people to believe that they can murder anyone who does not believe their barbaric and primitive religious tenets.

Religious Violence. The Crusades (the People's Crusade, the Northern Crusade, the Albigensian Crusade, and Crusades One through Nine).

The Inquisitions (Spanish, Portuguese, and Roman); witch hunts (the execution of tens of thousands of people, mostly women).

Christian conquistadors (extermination of native peoples by the millions); the interminable European Wars of Religion (the Nine Years War, the Thirty Years War, the Eighty Years War, the French Wars of Religion, the Wars of the Three Kingdoms, the English Civil War).

The American Civil War (in which Northern Christians and Southern Christians slaughtered one another over the issue of slavery).

The First World War (in which German Christians fought French, British, and American Christians, all of whom believed that God was on *their* side—German soldiers, for example, had *Gott mit uns—God with us*—embossed on their belt buckles.)

And that's just in the Western world.

There are the seemingly endless religious conflicts in Indonesia, India, Pakistan, Afghanistan, Iraq, Sudan, numerous countries in Africa, and of course Islamist terrorism.

Religious Intolerance. Religion kept the slave trade alive through religious and biblical arguments that blacks were inferior to whites, that slavery was good for black souls, that slavery gave blacks civilization, that blacks liked being enslaved, or, later, that blacks should not have the same civil rights as whites (such equal treatment under the law—interracial marriage was illegal until 1967) simply because the pigment in their skin was darker.

Religious Suppression. Religion has led otherwise good men to think that women should not have the same rights as they, which is what almost all Christians believed until the women's rights movement of the 20th century (and many today still believe in wanting to control women's sexuality and reproductive choices).

Like the meddling Puritanical control freaks of the Early Modern Period, there are still men today who think *they* should decide what women do with their vagina.

Women flourish in societies that are either not very religious or those, like the United States, that have separation of church and state; i.e., less religion equals more rights and equality.

Religious Moralizing. Religion has caused otherwise decent Christians to become perversely obsessed with what other people do with their genitals in the privacy of their bedrooms. And that if these people don't insert their genitals into the biblically correct orifice, or if genitals are stimulated in a biblically unapproved manner, they should not have the same Constitutional rights as straights.

Religious Xenophobia. The world's religions are tribal and xenophobic by nature, serving to regulate moral rules within the community but not seeking to embrace humanity outside their circle.

— *Part III - The Solution* —

Religion, by definition, forms an identity of *those like us*, in sharp distinction from *those not us, those heathens, those unbelievers.*

Religious Dogmatism. The foundation of the belief in an Absolute Morality is the belief in an Absolute Religion grounded in the One True God.

This inexorably leads to the conclusion that anyone who believes differently has departed from The Truth and thus is unprotected by our moral obligations; even more, they must be forced to see the Way, the Truth, and the Light.

Unlike science, religion has no systematic process and no empirical method to employ to determine the verisimilitude of its claims and beliefs, much less right and wrong, so it can never self-correct its mistakes, which are legion.

Religious Immorality. The morality of holy books—most notably the Bible—is not the morality any of us would wish to live by.

Put into historical context, the Bible's moral prescriptions were for another time for another people and have little relevance for us today.

In order to make the Bible relevant, believers must pick and choose biblical passages that suit their needs.

Thus, the game of cherry picking from the Bible generally works to the advantage of the cherry pickers.

SACREDNESS: A NEW UNDERSTANDING

WE ADVANCE TECHNOLOGICALLY BUT NOT SOCIALLY, POLITICALLY, OR INTELLECTUALLY

We advance technologically with ease but not so socially, politically, or intellectually.
We war with each other in every way conceivable.
We destroy our environment and deplete our resources.
Why is that?

We don't drive around in vehicles that are thousands of years old.
We don't see chariots being driven down our streets.
Yet, we cling to belief systems, religions, that are thousands of years old.
These religions are products of the infancy of our intelligence.

As a consequence, many of us exist in a world of fiction and fantasy.
We do not understand our reality and its behavioral demands.
We do not recognize the inherent value in our diversity.

Instead, full of fear, we create all kinds of divisions, all kinds of tribes.

We have nation-state tribes, political-party tribes, religious tribes, corporate tribes, ad infinitum.

And we war with each other.

As a consequence, we exist not more secure but less secure.

We have created a destructive and unsustainable momentum that must be arrested and reversed if we are going to improve the quality of our lives, end our needless suffering, prosper together, find peace, sustain humanity, and advance our civilization.

We need a reality-based understanding of what is sacred in our world and cannot, at our peril, be violated, damaged, dishonored, or destroyed.

INFANCY OF OUR INTELLIGENCE

When I was a child, my family, as Catholics, attended church regularly.

I served countless masses as an altar boy.

It was my nature at a very young age, as it has been all my life, to be observant and contemplative.

I observed the restrained and reverential behavior of people in church.

They crossed themselves with "holy" water as they entered.

During the service, they bowed, genuflected, stood, kneeled, and prayed in reverent obedience.

I also observed outside the church the irreverent, insensitive, and sometimes brutal behavior of these same sanctimonious people.

I thought to myself, "There is something wrong here."

At that young age, I did not yet know the word hypocrisy.

As I continued to observe life, I was struck by how we complicated it unnecessarily.

I thought to myself, "Life is not this complicated. Why do we make it more difficult than it is?"

Wherever I went, as the years passed, I observed similar hypocritical and disturbing behavioral patterns.

I went on to live a very unusual life of many rich and diverse experiences in a variety of fields.

Later in life, I studied at two of the world's most renowned divinity schools, Yale and Harvard.

At the latter, as noted earlier, I earned a Master of Divinity degree.

I went to these schools to study ethics, global environmental problems, and world religious belief systems.

Simultaneously, on my own, I studied cosmology and evolutionary biology.

I went to continue on the learning track I had been on all my life.

I was fifty years old the year I graduated from Harvard.
As an older student, I remained objective in my study and analysis of world religions.
I studied all the major world religions.

While they are all interesting and rich in history and rituals, one finds that they remain human constructs formed thousands of years ago in the infancy of our intelligence by people like you and me.
The historical context and ancient mindsets that produced these belief systems are abundantly evident.
Clearly, they are all a part of our very early efforts to understand and cope with the withering and unrelenting demands of life.
As such, they should be treated like all other institutions that we have created.
Now, ancient and antiquated, these religions should be studied as history not adopted as belief systems.

No disparagement or disrespect is meant.
I appreciate the good efforts of all those who have preceded us honorably.
We are no different than they in our quest for life's ultimate answers.
But as Gandhi observed, "Religious ideas are subject to the same laws of evolution that govern everything else in the universe."
In other words, there comes a time to let go of dated ideas and advance as life demands just as we do in every other field of endeavor.

— Part III - The Solution —

The study of religion, costly in time and funds, was a liberating and rewarding experience.

It cleared my mind of the false religious dogma that as a child I was programmed—literally brainwashed by the Catholic church—to believe.

Just as children continue to be today.

That clearance was the second most valuable benefit I derived from my divinity school experience.

The most valuable benefit was the discovery, step by step, on my own, of that for which I was searching.

It happened like this:

With a cleared mind, I compared and contrasted our present circumstances with our ancient past.

To paraphrase sociologist Lester Milbrath, over time we have developed a complex and integrated social, technical, economic, and military system so powerful that we can dominate and destroy each other and the rest of the natural world.

Alongside it, we have retained an ethical system based on very old ideas.

Ancient western religions would have us believe that a god exists as a monarch, rules over a kingdom, is distant from the world, relates primarily to humans, and saves whatever he chooses, thus relieving us of our responsibility to save ourselves and other living things.

Science, on the other hand, explains our physical world but provides no moral guidance for living within it.

The lack of congruence between our major inherited religions and the power and exuberance of our modern world is gravely problematic.

This is a reality that most of us choose to deny, or one of which we are unaware, and one that is perpetuated by clinging to ancient notions of what is sacred.

In a brilliant statement, some twenty-six hundred years ago, the Buddha said, "To insist on a spiritual practice that served us in the past is to carry the raft on our back after we have crossed the river."

Having crossed the river myself, so to speak, it was time for me to examine the concept of sacredness.

A modern belief system must be based on a current understanding of what is sacred.

But who is to say what is sacred, the scientist or the priest? Where does the truth lie?

Dr. Clinton Lee Scott wrote, and I paraphrase and agree, that no one person or category of people has the inside track on truth.

Truth may be discovered by scientists, poets, prophets, housewives, garage mechanics, so forth.

And always by the way of human experience.

Truths are derived by men and women, not cloistered from the world, but who live in it with all the temptations, problems, and perplexities common in the daily round of human existence.

It is here, in our daily lives at home, in the community, and in the world—not in creeds and doctrines however long ago proclaimed—where we find the way of life, the architecture of life, *the way life works*.

SPIRITUAL

Many of us say we do not like organized religion but that we are "spiritual."
There is something about the word that feels right to many people.
But what does the word "spiritual" really mean?
Our world has taken enormous liberties with this word.

Religious groups engage in "holy wars," a play on words so egregious, that it gives new meaning to the word oxymoron.
Atrocious acts of terrorism are committed.
For example, a busload, café, or office building full of innocent people, to include children, is firebombed.
Those who are responsible claim to be spiritually motivated.

If each person in a group were asked to define the word "spiritual," each, and understandably so, would have a different definition.
What does this word mean?

Spiritual may be defined as having to do with sacred matters or sacred things.
We have arrived at the word "sacred."
It sounds wonderful.
But what, in a religious sense, does it mean?

Sacred may be defined as that which is associated with gods or that which is associated with religion.
When we say that sacred is that which is associated with gods, the question arises immediately, "What and whose god or goddess are we talking about?"

Most people have different ideas about the concept of a god or gods.
Seldom, and understandably so, is there agreement.

When we attempt to define or worship these gods, we create religious problems.
Definitions are divisive and invite conflicts.

Historically, we have had and, to this day, continue to have conflicts.

Worship of these gods is diversionary and distracting.
Our attention gets focused "out there" somewhere, worshipping something we have been programmed to believe exists, is sacred, and by which we are going to be "saved."

We are going to be saved even though we live horribly unhealthy lives, go to war with our neighbors literally and figuratively, destroy our environment, and deplete our resources.
Yet, we are going to be saved.
It doesn't make sense which is common in the world of religion.
Another understanding of sacred is that which is associated with religion.

We have gone from spiritual having to do with sacred, to sacred having to do with religion.
We haven't gotten very far.
The obvious question is, "*What is religion?*"

Religion may be defined as a belief in, or worship of, a god.
That definition takes us back to gods.
Immediately, the same problematic questions arise:
What and whose gods or goddesses?
The conflicts over definitions of gods and goddesses.

— *Part III - The Solution* —

The diversion and distraction of our attention to these supernatural gods and goddesses.

Religion may also be defined as a belief system that has to do with the cause, purpose, and nature of life and the universe.

In fact, this is what we did long before the Scientific Revolution and the Enlightenment (also known as the Age of Reason).

To explain the cause, purpose, and nature of life and the universe, men and women, priests and priestesses, profoundly ignorant of life as we know it today, often claiming "divine revelation" (i.e., communication with gods and other supernatural entities) as their source of inspiration, knowledge, and authority, created gods, creation stories, texts, and fiercely tribal religions with rules, rituals, costumes, and music.

It's essential to be clear on how very old the major religions are. Recall that Hinduism began about 6,000 years ago, Judaism about 4,000 years ago, Buddhism, Confucianism, and Taoism about 2,600 years ago, Christianity about 2,000 years ago, and Islam about 1,400 years ago.

All these religions formed thousands of years before the Scientific Revolution and the Enlightenment when, in the 16th to 18th centuries, a mere 300 to 500 years ago, mathematics, physics, chemistry, astronomy, biology, and anatomy put forth a range of ideas based on reason as the primary source of authority and legitimacy.

Religious creeds, doctrines, and dogma were questioned, and the authority of religions were challenged.

All for very good reasons.

Today, we do not need "divine revelation" to explain the cause, purpose, and nature of life and the universe.

The generally accepted theory for the *cause* of the universe is the Big Bang.

We don't have a clue what the *purpose* of the universe is or if it has a purpose.

We understand only a very small portion of the universe.

All the stars, planets, and galaxies that we can see comprise just four percent of the universe.
The other 96 percent is made of stuff astronomers can't see, detect, or even comprehend.

As noted, when we look into the sky on a very clear and starry night, we think we are looking at the universe.
In fact, we are looking at about 2,500 stars of the 200 to 400 billion stars in the Milky Way galaxy, one of trillions of galaxies and dwarf galaxies in the universe.

And, the universe is growing larger, expanding, faster than the speed of light.
Faster than 186,000 miles per second, faster than a billion miles per hour!
Creating more stars at an estimated 4,800 per second!
After the birth and death of stars, the net gain is about 275 million a day!
And more galaxies!

In our galaxy alone, the Milky Way, astronomers estimate that there are about *100 billion* habitable Earth-like planets!

The purpose of all of this?
We don't have a clue.

However, *the nature of life and the universe* is another matter. It is here where the enigma unravels.
Here, in reality, in the nature of life and the universe, is where the architecture of life and true sacredness (nonreligious) are revealed.

True sacredness is that in life which, at our peril, we cannot violate, damage, dishonor, or destroy.

SACRED CONSTRUCT

Philosopher Arthur Schopenhauer observed that all truth passes through three stages.
First, it is ridiculed.
Second, it is violently opposed.
Third, it is accepted as self-evident.

Such a truth has emerged in our lifetime.
It informs us that we exist as a tiny fragment of an immensely larger interlocking whole in which all of the parts are interconnected and dependent upon each other for survival.
Allow me to repeat that.
A truth has emerged that informs us that we exist as a tiny fragment of an immensely larger interlocking whole in which *all of the parts are interconnected and dependent upon each other for survival.*

Simply put, everything is connected to everything else.
We exist, not separately, but in communion with all living things.
Life is an interrelated, interdependent phenomenon.
That is the nature of the universe.
That is the nature of life.
Everything is in relationship.

"So, what." One might respond, and ask, "What is the practical value of that?"
It's a reasonable question.
The practical value lies in the realization that there are several relationships that are foundational.
These are the foundational relationships of our lives.

These are three relationships out of which all other relationships follow.

The first is our relationship with our self.

The second is our relationship with others.

The third is our relationship with our environment.

If we chose one word to describe what optimizes each of these relationships, our relationship with our self is about *health*.
Our relationship with others is about *kindness*.
Our relationship with our environment is about *respect*.

Our Foundational Relationships

Self – Health
Others – Kindness
Environment – Respect

The quality of our lives reflects the quality of these relationships. This is a sacred construct that exists as an integral part of reality. This is not a human construct.

Why do I write that this is a sacred construct?
It is because *these relationships represent that in life which, at our peril, we cannot violate, damage, dishonor, or destroy.*

When we violate these relationships, we suffer.
This is simply the way life works.
This is not contrived or fiction.
It's not arbitrary or subject to dismissal.
It's not in any way negotiable.
It has nothing to do with gods, religions, or anything supernatural.

— *Part III - The Solution* —

How we take care of ourselves, each other, and our environment determines not only the quality of our lives but whether we will live or die.

These relationships are sacred.
They are the wellsprings of life.
We emerged from these relationships.
We are sustained by them.

We are surrounded by the very sacredness that, historically, we have sought from afar.

This understanding of sacredness must be recognized and addressed as a dynamic reality that is forever being discovered.
It's not unchanging and vested in the past like archaic dogma.
Always, we continue to refine our understanding of how to optimize these three foundational relationships: how to better care for ourselves, relate to each other, and nurture our environment.

It's as Greek philosopher Heraclitus observed, "You cannot step into the same river twice."
Why is that? It is because the river is forever flowing and changing.
Yet, it remains the same river.

Similarly, our understanding of what optimizes these relationships flows out of a stream of knowledge that continually changes.
These foundational relationships will always exist.
Our understanding of how to optimize them evolves as our knowledge grows.

The spirit, from the Latin word spiritus for breath, that animates life exists in, expresses itself through, and is sustained by these foundational relationships.
These are the vessels of life.

When we destroy any of these relationships—our health, our relationships with others, or our environment—we extinguish the spirit, the breath, of life.

When we destroy these relationships, there is no place left through which the phenomenon that we call life can express itself, can breathe.

The vitality is gone as it is for anyone who cannot breathe.

To live a spiritual life (*if one wants to call it that*), or a reverent life—to breathe—is to honor these three relationships in all their manifestations.

This is the much sought-after key to the concept of *sustainability*: the understanding that we must leave this planet as we found it or improve it so those generations that follow us will have the same, or better, opportunities that we have had.

This is a daunting challenge given that we add about 75 million people a year to our planet.

That is an addition of about 1,500,000 people *each week* to feed, clothe, house, educate, employ, transport, govern, protect and keep healthy.

The key to sustainability is to take the word apart.

Make two words of it: sustain ability, i.e., our ability to sustain these three foundational relationships: our health, our relationships with others, and the health of our environment.

How do we do that?

To do it, we have to identify our *responsibilities*.

So often, it's asked, "What is the purpose or the meaning of life?"

These questions send us in circles.

The appropriate question is, "What are the responsibilities of life?"

The answer, again, lies in taking the word apart and making two words of it: response abilities.

— *Part III - The Solution* —

We must develop our abilities to respond to life's challenges and stimuli so as to optimize and sustain our three foundational relationships.

This understanding of sacredness does not mandate worship but responsibility.
Right living is about behavior, not worship.
Salvation, saving ourselves from harm or loss, is not delivered by a supreme being, it is earned by us.
The forgiveness of our "sins" lies not in the hands of some external god.
It's found in our alignment with the uncompromising demands of the reality in which we exist.

At this time in our evolution, this understanding of sacredness is easily within our perception and grasp.

CRITICAL MIND SHIFT

In his book, *The World's Religions*, Houston Smith writes of the two issues on which most religions agree.

They all advise adherence to some version of the Golden Rule and avoidance of self-centeredness.

Generally, we do neither one.

Self-centered and shameless, we too often do to others and our environment whatever we can get away with.

We get by with this behavior in the short term.

In time, we find that we are victims of our own exploitation.

For the way of life, the architecture of life, reveals an exquisite intimacy among all phenomena.

Life also broadcasts a riveting truth from which there is no escape.

I call it *the reverse side of the Golden Rule.*

The Golden Rule commands that we do to others as we would have others do to us.

The reverse side of the Golden Rule does not command anything.

It warns that *what we do to others we do to ourselves.*

In an interconnected world, all exploitation and oppression inevitably returns to its source.

This is a reality that we must understand, and from this understanding make the critical mind-shift required of us if we are to sustain humanity and advance our civilization.

This mind shift is to understand clearly, unequivocally, that what we do to others we do to ourselves.

This is evident in our foundational relationships.
In each there exists a dynamic between self and other.

Consider our relationship with our environment.
If we damage and destroy our environment, we damage and destroy ourselves.

In our relationships with other people, if we mistreat and/or are unkind to others, our actions return to haunt and torment us in one form or another over time.

In our relationship with ourselves, if we abuse ourself, our health, in any one of countless ways, sooner or later, we will suffer the consequences.

When all of this becomes evident and acted upon, our belief system and behavior become fused and aligned, not with some fantasy or fictional story, but with the reality in which we exist.
Our belief system is not just something for one day of the week, or a particular time of the day when we pray or bow to this or that god, or to be celebrated in special places only.
Our belief system becomes our lifestyle, and our lifestyle becomes aligned with and honors the larger reality in which we exist.

Often, we are confronted by well-meaning "religious" people who read, quote from, and thump their "holy" books.
These people are everywhere: television, radio, newspapers, magazines, Internet, and billboards.
They even knock on our doors to evangelize and proselytize.

In interacting with these people, it often becomes evident that many don't know how to take of care of their health, how to get along with their neighbors, or understand our fragile relationship with our environment.

— *Part III - The Solution* —

One feels like saying to them, "Some of what you have in your book is fine, but what is going on in the rest of your life?"

Many of us have been taught that a creator has "endowed" us with "free will."
This ingenious bit of theological inventiveness, among so many others, was designed to relieve gods of the responsibility for having created the dark side of life.
Gods get the credit for all the good things.
We, because of "free will," get the blame for all the bad.

This is a very clever construction.
That aside, do we really have free will?
Yes, of course.
Like all other creatures, we can do whatever we like.

We can lead unhealthy lifestyles.
We can mistreat and exploit others.
We can pollute our air, water, and soil and deplete and destroy our resources.

In other words, we can and do destroy the foundational relationships of our lives.
We have free will.

But we do not have free will over the consequences.
We cannot will the consequences.
In an interrelated, interdependent world, the consequences—like the outcome of a mathematical equation—are fixed.

Our only choice, in fact, is to honor the way of life as it really is and prosper or violate the way of life and suffer needlessly.

Sacredness is not a complex, difficult, and esoteric thing to understand.

It is found in real life relationships here and now, not out there somewhere.

Sacredness is not about a Supreme Being. It's about a way of being.

The focus of our beliefs must shift from what was imagined to exist and be sacred in some heavenly realm to what does exist and is sacred here and now.

It is time to find our comfort not in the worship of distant mythological gods, but in present, real-life relationships with each other, with our extraordinary environment, and in our own unique individuality.

These "commandments" are not issued by a god, but by the undeniable reality of our existence.
Certainly, the fictional gods of our historical religions would approve of this shift of emphasis.
When we take care of ourselves and each other, and leave our environment as we found it or improve it, we are living a sacred life.

One would think that if there exists anything benevolent in dimensions beyond our perception—call it a god, creator, supreme being, the force, universal intelligence, divine consciousness, or whatever—that it, she, him, or them would cheer us wildly when the focus of our lives is on health for ourselves, kindness toward each other, and respect for our environment.

For what more could any god of any belief system anywhere ask of us?

THREE SIMPLE RULES

Many of us are familiar with the Ten Commandments that appear in Exodus, the second book of the Bible, written some thirty-three hundred years ago.

What do these commandments say?

The first four have to do with a god and the Sabbath.
The remaining six are about behavior.
We are told to honor our parents and to not murder, steal, lie, commit adultery, or covet.

We would all agree that we have learned a few things in the last thirty-three hundred years.

It may be that instead of the Ten Commandments, we require just three simple rules for living that say and do more than these ten.

If we followed these three simple rules—*seven words*—we would eliminate the majority of problems and suffering in our world, problems that the Ten Commandments don't address.

None of these three rules appear in the Ten Commandments.

The first is *be healthy.*
Each of us is like a cell in the body of humanity.
The health of all of us taken together determines the health of humanity and our civilization.

The bodies and minds that we occupy may be the most exquisite "machines" on the planet.

The abuse to which we subject them, we wouldn't dream of doing to our material possessions like our cars, computers, or homes.

Yet, our bodies and minds are our homes.

Perhaps the reason that we don't value them more is that we get them for free.

We are given this most prized possession at birth.

By the time we realize their value, for many of us, it is very late, if not too late.

Be healthy.

When we are healthy, it is easier to follow the second simple rule.

The second rule is *be kind*.

The Ten Commandments tell us to honor our parents, which is fine.

Aside from that, they tell us not what to do but what not to do: not to murder, steal, lie, commit adultery, or covet.

In all our relationships, what we need to do is simply be kind.

We need to treat each other, our friends and neighbors, better.

We must stop exploiting each other.

It does not matter how much money we have or earn, what size home we live in, what kind of car we drive, how many academic degrees we may have accumulated, what accomplishments we may have achieved, or what our title or position is.

Nor does it matter what our gender, race, religion, age, appearance, national origin, sexual orientation, or political affiliation is.

What matters is whether or not we are kind to one another.

The third simple rule is *respect the environment.*

In every conceivable way, we are linked to our environment.

We evolved from it.

Everything comes from our environment.

If we destroy our environment, we destroy ourselves.

In time, our damaged environment and ecological systems will regenerate but we will be gone.

Nature, which couldn't care less about humanity, will have eliminated us.

— *Part III - The Solution* —

It's that simple.
Three rules, seven words.
When we follow them, our lives change.
As many of our lives change, our world changes.

Be healthy.
Be kind.
Respect the environment.

If you wish to astonish the whole world, tell people that—the simple truth.

THE FOUNDATIONAL RELATIONSHIPS

THE LAW OF ONE

Many of us are ready for a belief system grounded in reality that actually promotes universal harmony.

It is apparent that we live in a world where we are destructive to ourselves, each other, and the environment that enables us to exist.

The belief system I describe emerges from the awareness and comprehension of the oneness in which we exist and the sacredness of the relationships by which it is sustained.

The unwritten Law of One informs us that all that exists is a part of and is affected by everything else that exists.

This "law" acknowledges and honors the dynamic equilibrium among all life forms.

It recognizes the existence of universal principles: oneness, diversity, interrelatedness, individuality, and interdependence.

Universal Principles

Oneness: All that exists is a part of and is affected by everything else that exists.

Diversity: The whole is comprised of an infinite number of diverse parts.

Interrelatedness: All parts are interrelated.

Individuality: All parts are unique.

Interdependence: All parts depend upon each other for survival These principles confirm that our reality is a product of an infinite number of diverse, unique, interrelated, and interdependent parts.

An understanding of these principles yields virtues such as *reverence, universal benevolence, and sustainable industry.*

This understanding changes forever the way we think about and conduct our relationships with ourselves, with each other, and with our environment.
It explains how we have created our problems and provides clear direction on how we can change.
It calls for individual responsibility and initiative.

In this realm of understanding lies the treasures associated with our higher potential.
These are treasures in the fullest sense.
For within their realization lies the fate of humankind and many other species.

The simple truth is the way of life as it really is.
It is reality, not myth or superstition.
If we honor it, we prosper.
If we violate it, we suffer and condemn our future to adversity.

All of life—*the way of life*—is about relationships.

The foundational relationships of life are with self, others, and our environment.

We complicate life unnecessarily.

We need simply to be healthy, be kind, and respect our environment.

"Be healthy, be kind, and respect our environment" is not enough for most people.

They want specific instructions.

Knowledgeable people worldwide have amassed an enormous amount of information about how to care for ourselves, relate to others, and respect our environment.

In our age of information and communication, this constantly updated information is available freely and disseminated nonstop.

We need only to access and incorporate it into our lives.

Our forbearers never had it so easy.

As an introduction, let me offer the following thoughts about each of our foundational relationships.

RELATIONSHIP WITH SELF

Be Healthy

In a word, our relationship with our self is about *health*—physical, mental, and emotional.

We are each a cell of the body we call humanity.
The health and vitality of humanity can be neither more nor less than the sum total of us taken together.
Our civilization hinges on the state of our personal and collective health.

Each of us is responsible for our own health. We can choose to live a healthy lifestyle.
Conversely, we can abuse our health in whatever manner we choose until finally we succumb to the ravages of an unhealthy lifestyle.

Each of us is the person over which we have the most control.
When the errors of our ways shout at us, it is absurd for us to repeat them.
We can change our lifestyle.
Rarely, can we change another person's lifestyle.

Life cannot be violated beyond a critical point before its systems begin to disintegrate and fail.
That applies to our personal health as well as to the health of our planet.

It's unfortunate when, due to circumstances beyond our control, we are unable to be healthy fully.

It is, however, tragic for us to not be healthy, body and mind, when we have a choice.

A healthy lifestyle is easy.

And rewarding.

We are the gatekeepers of our bodies and minds.

It is one of the rare things in life over which we have near total control.

"Do no harm" is a fundamental principle in healthcare.

The same measure, do no harm, should be our guide to what foods and drinks we put into our bodies and what thoughts we allow into our minds.

All of this input contributes to what we might call our *health account*.

Our health account is similar to, but more important ultimately than, a bank account that we contribute to for our financial health.

Our health account is an accumulation of all that we do to support and enhance our health.

There are very many people with healthy bank accounts that wish they would have given the same attention to their health accounts.

They often discover this too late.

For physical health, we need to engage in moderate but regular physical activities of our choice.

Our bodies require movement.

A simple program of regular physical activity and wise food and drink choices will yield—with very little effort—enormous results for a lifetime.

— Part III - The Solution —

If we are born with limitations, or incur them, we can still optimize our potential as so many who are handicapped in one way or another demonstrate.

Too many of us dig our graves with our knives and forks.

The remedy is not a diet but a shift to a lifestyle that is healthy.

People resist change to a healthy lifestyle fearful that they must give up what they cherish.

Ironically, those who embrace healthy changes find to their amazement only that they have improved their lives and have given up nothing but problems.

A healthy relationship with food and drink is an enormous challenge for many people.

It need not be.

It is simple matter that comes down to the *quality and quantity* of food and drink that we consume.

As for *quality*, we require wholesome foods such as fruits, vegetables, whole grains, beans, nuts, seeds, lean meats, fowl, fish, and olive oil, for examples.

There are countless ways to combine and prepare healthy foods into meals at least as delicious as anything of lesser quality.

These foods that pass through us are what nourishes are bodies.

Why settle for less when consuming healthy foods and drinks is a win-win for health, taste, budget, and the reduction of medical costs?

As for *quantity*, each of us, in a sense, is allotted so many calories daily.

For an average woman and man, it's about 2,000 and 2,500 calories per day respectively.

It's like a gift.

We can spend these calories as we like.

If we consume our full allotment of calories, our weight remains unchanged.

If we consume more, we gain weight.

If we consume less, we lose weight.

If we engage in more than normal physical activity, we expend additional calories.

It's very simple.

Our appetites for and enjoyment of food are like another gift.

Several times a day, we experience hunger which we satisfy with food and drink at breakfast, lunch, and dinner.

Several tasty and healthy meals a day within our daily allotment of calories should satisfy anyone.

Each day, we begin anew with our allotment of calories to spend and our appetite to satisfy with delicious foods and drinks.

Eating and drinking well—quality and quantity—and regular moderate physical activity yields healthy bodies.

But there's more.

It is also critical to understand the indispensable role that sleep plays in our mental and physical health and the quality of our lives.

Sleep, like exercise and nutrition, is a biological necessity.

Give sleep the importance that it deserves.

It plays a vital role in every aspect of our health and in every dimension and waking moment of our lives.

Take time to rest adequately.

It is time well spent, as much so as any other healthy endeavor in which we invest.

What else can be noted about a healthy mind?

Particularly in a highly competitive, often chaotic, and stressful world in which all life forms strive and compete to survive and reproduce.

— *Part III - The Solution* —

The achievement of a healthy and peaceful mind is a far more complicated challenge than a healthy body.

Throughout the ages, countless teachers have addressed and continue to address this dimension of life.
Many of them compete with each other for your attention and money.
One could spend many lifetimes reading their recommendations. None of us have the time to sift through it all.

What is the essence of wisdom?
After more than seven decades of rich and diverse experiences in an array of fields and the acquisition of a couple of advanced degrees from fine universities, I would say that the essence of wisdom is to get grounded in the extraordinary phenomenon known as *reality*.
Pay attention.
Endeavor to see and understand life as it is.

In human interactions, we find trickery and virtue everywhere.
It's normal.
Keep it all in perspective.
Rudyard Kipling summed it up beautifully in his poem "If."

As for making personal life changes, a *firm decision* is required to trigger the process.
Otherwise, the effort is doomed at the start.
There is a well-known quote by German writer and statesman Johann Goethe, "Whatever you can do, or dream you can begin it. Boldness has genius power and magic to it. Begin it now."
Most people who are familiar with this inspiring quote are unaware that this is just the end of the quote.

The part that precedes it is even more insightful:
"Until one is committed, there is hesitancy, the chance to draw back, always ineffectiveness.

"Concerning all acts of initiative (and creation), there is one elementary truth (the ignorance of which kills countless ideas and splendid plans).

"That is the moment one definitely commits oneself, then providence moves too.

"All sorts of things occur to help one that would have never otherwise occurred.

"*A whole stream of events issues from the decision,* raising in one's favor all manner of unforeseen incidents and meetings and material assistance which no person could have dreamed would have come his way."

In other words, *decide and commit.*

Make a plan and execute it.

When you do, you will be astonished at what follows.

Our *Relationship with Self* is our first and core foundational relationship.

It determines our physical and mental health and, as a consequence, affects our relationships with other people and our environment.

Let me share the following with you as it relates to living a healthy life.

Many years ago, I wrote a book entitled *Russell, Alexandra and John.*

Russell is a wise teacher, an ageless sage.

Alexandra and John, twin youngsters, befriend Russell and seek his advice about life.

In response to one of the questions from John, Russell offered the following:

"High priests and priestesses are not in short supply these days.

"One has quite a varied menu of both teachers and teachings from which to choose.

Part III - The Solution

"It's remarkable that so many claim exclusive possession of the truth.

"Surely, they cannot all possess this most exclusive treasure.

"Many people are inclined and content to adopt a creed or fall under the spell of some charismatic personality.

"It is the result of a persistent human need for clarity and a leader who will show the way.

"As a consequence, you are overwhelmed with purveyors of many varieties of dogma vying with each other for followers, financial support, and power.

"The path that was to have led to liberation leads then only to another cell in the prison block, another blocked corridor in the maze.

"The purity and simplicity of that which was sought is lost to needless complexities, adornment, and exploitation.

"I do not claim to possess the truth, perhaps some truths.
"I do not claim to know the way, perhaps a way.
"I do not claim to have the answers, perhaps some answers.

"Go deep into the well that is you and seek the teacher within.
"Challenge belief systems.
"Challenge authority.
"Live life in the present, fairly and honorably.

"See the beauty in simplicity.
"Treat others as you wish to be treated.
"Respect your environment.
"Avoid self-centeredness.

"Fill your life with quality in the fulfillment of your genuine needs.

"Seek and experience learning but avoid teachings that are divisive.

"In all these things, be who are.

"Express your individuality, the beautiful imprint that is you uniquely.

"Trust yourself.

"Keep life simple.

"Don't be misguided, for there are those who would dazzle you with their costumes, settings, and rituals.

"I would suggest that the truth that you seek, elegant in its simplicity, is without need of adornment.

"There are those who would have you believe there is but one path that leads to peace.

"I would suggest that at the point where all paths converge, there begins the final leg of the journey to peace.

"There are those who would limit you with a rigid set of rules that restrict, bind, and diminish you, and then they modify these as convenience and events dictate.

"I would suggest that you avoid rigidity, but rather align yourself with that which is fluid, spontaneous, and you.

"There are those who would define you primarily as a spirit and have you focus your attention on your next life.

"I would suggest that you acknowledge, experience, and celebrate the reality of your current life which is far from an illusion.

"There are those who would have you follow and serve them as their disciples.

"I would suggest that you follow yourself as all have equal access to the source of inspiration.

"Learn only from those who seek, not to bind you, but to set you free."

RELATIONSHIPS WITH OTHERS

Be Kind

There are billions of us on planet Earth.
We add about 75 million people to our population each year—*nearly a million and a half a week, more than 200,000 each day!*

Our relationships with each other, as individuals and nation states, have always been and continue to be troubled.
Why?
It's likely because of inherited behavior derived from our ancient short-term survival instincts.

These protective behavioral responses, hard-wired, still frame how the minds of many of us work today.
Getting past this genetic programming may be humanity's greatest challenge if we are to sustain our existence and advance our civilization.

Too often, we act only in our perceived self-interest.
We feel that if we do not look out for ourselves, who will?
In today's intimately interrelated world, we are obliged to look beyond ourselves.
In our interdependent existence, we ignore and mistreat others at our peril.

We are like links in a chain.
The fate of each link, directly and indirectly, affects all the others.
There is individuality but not independence.
To think differently is to delude ourselves.
We are dependent upon each other at every turn.

Each person's health and integrity affects the health and integrity of the whole.

We are each a part of a system of relationships that embrace our family, friends, neighbors, business associates, organizations, communities, nations, and family of nations.
No single object or entity exists independently.
What we do to others, we do to ourselves.

My late brother, Russell, a graduate of the U.S. Military Academy at West Point, in his later years, posted a note near his desk in his Washington, D.C. office: "Everyone tells the truth."
The reality, and what my brother understood, is that *everyone tells their truth.*
As a result, where two are more gather there will be disagreement.
It's a fact of life.
The evidence is overwhelming.
Our greatest challenge in all of our infinite endeavors is to find common ground peacefully in our relationships with others.

Above and beyond finding common ground with others is *kindness*, an extraordinary and powerful quality.
So much so that when we witness exceptional acts of kindness, tears come to our eyes.
Instinctively, we recognize that something wonderful and selfless has occurred.
Kindness is an expression of our nurturing dimension.
It is human nature at its best.
This is something each of us has the opportunity to demonstrate in large and small ways daily.

Most people carry heavy burdens.
Life is not easy.
Help to lighten their load.
Be kind.
You will be rewarded richly even though you do not seek a reward.

RELATIONSHIP WITH OUR ENVIRONMENT

Respect Our Environment

In a word, our relationship with our environment is about *respect*.
We live on a planet soaring through space.
We call this spacecraft Earth.

It is a spacecraft (Earth) within a spacecraft (solar system) within a spacecraft (Milky Way galaxy) within a spacecraft (universe).
Our universe may be another spacecraft within a multiverse.

As Edward O. Wilson wrote, "Humanity did not descend as angelic beings into this world.
"Nor are we aliens who colonized Earth.
"We evolved here, one among many species, across millions of years, and exist as an organic miracle linked to others.

"The natural environment we treat with such unnecessary ignorance and recklessness was our cradle and nursery, our school, and remains our one and only home.
"To its special conditions, we are intimately adapted in every one of the bodily fibers and bio-chemical transactions that gives us life."

We are a product of this tiny orb that is our world.
Over billions of years, we have evolved and emerged in concert with other species of plants and animals.

As a part of this whole, we are subject to the natural laws that enable everything to exist.

Every physical thing we require and enjoy is derived from our world.

Everything.

Every breath we breathe, every drop we drink, and every bite of food is derived from our environment.

Every bit of clothing, medicine, building material, and everything else is drawn from this source.

This world gave birth to us and countless other species of plants and animals.

Now, much of life, including our own, is threatened.

We are polluting and decimating life-support systems, plundering resources, and driving species to extinction.

The rate and range of global environmental deterioration is unprecedented.

It is driven by the relentless needs of a global population that has grown out of control.

Author John Gray pointed out in *Straw Dogs*, "The destruction of the natural world is not the result of global capitalism, industrialization, 'Western civilization' or any flaw in human institutions.

"It is a consequence of the evolutionary success of an exceptionally rapacious primate.

"Throughout all of history and prehistory, human advance has coincided with ecological devastation."

Parasite-like and swarming, we are destroying our environment.

With astonishing speed, we are attacking our ecosystems like businesses in liquidation.

We have upset an extraordinary array of life that took billions of years and endless experiments to produce.

— Part III - The Solution —

Environmental problems cross the boundaries of nation states, academic disciplines, political and cultural ideologies, and religious theologies.

They affect the affluent and the impoverished, developed and developing nations, individuals and whole societies.

These problems are far more than just another on a list of major concerns.

Our relationship with our environment is at the core of our existence.

Our relationship with our ecosystems is sacred and inviolable.
At our peril, we cannot violate, damage, or destroy them.

Nowhere do we find clearer and unmistakable evidence that what we do to others, we do to ourselves than in our relationship with our biosphere—Earth and its atmosphere where life and we exist.

Respect our environment.

It's the only one we have.

OUR COMPETING SETS OF SURVIVAL INSTINCTS

Be healthy.
Be kind.
Respect the environment.

Seven words.
Sounds simple enough.
Why don't we do it?

We don't do it because we have competing sets of survival instincts.

Our competing sets of survival instincts produce opposing worldviews, beliefs, impulses, and actions that account for the epic struggle daily for the evolution and survival of humanity.

Our competing sets of survival instincts are the products of evolution

Our first set of survival instincts is perfectly normal, natural, organic, and . . . disastrous.

These are our short-term survival instincts.

Like all creatures, we are programmed, genetically predisposed, hardwired, to make it to tomorrow, i.e., to survive and reproduce.

These short-term survival instincts generate behavior that is characterized by fear, greed, power, control, immediate gratification, self-centeredness, authoritarianism, denial of inequality, and the like.

This is a set of survival instincts—essential in primitive times to survive—that now retards our evolution

Evolution has also given us another set of survival instincts, our long-term survival instincts.

These occur as a result of our large and evolved brains.

Among all vertebrates, relative to size, we have the largest brains.

Unique among all species, we are able to reflect on our behavior and project to where our behavior is taking us.

To where our behavior is taking us is not a pretty picture.

We are like an airplane flying overhead with someone out on the wing popping rivets until the plane crashes.

We are beginning to understand that our short-term survival instincts and related behavior are destroying us.

We want to survive for the long-term, not the short-term.

We want to improve the quality of our lives, sustain humanity, and advance our civilization.

The word "sustainability" has come into wide usage.

It is the understanding that we must leave this planet as we found it or improve it so those who follow us will have the same or better opportunities that we have had.

We are a species, likely the first on this planet, who has an opportunity to advance beyond short-term survival instincts.

We are beginning to understand that our behavior cannot be characterized by fear, greed, power, control, immediate gratification, self-centeredness, authoritarianism, denial of inequalities, and the like.

Instead, our behavior must be characterized by health in all of its dimensions: physical, mental, and emotional.

By kindness toward each other and other nation-states.

By respect for our environment, our ecological systems, and our biosphere as we inhabit a very narrow and fragile band within our solar system that allows life to exist at all.

Our long-term survival instincts and associated behavior can sustain humanity and advance our civilization.

Each of these sets of survival instincts—the older short-term instincts and our emerging long-term instincts—generates powerful belief systems in the areas of politics, business, social interaction, and religion.

Politics

Our old short-term survival instincts generate politics that is adversarial, hostile and belligerent.

It's about the destruction of one's *perceived* opposition whether that is an individual, organization, or a nation-state.

It is politics that favors unilateralism and unjustified pre-emptive wars.

Our long-term survival instincts and emerging worldview favor non-adversarial politics.

It's about finding the common ground.

It is a worldview that recognizes that we don't have the time, resources, or energy to fight with each other.

And, that we have severe and complicated problems on our planet—social, political, economic, and environmental—that must be addressed urgently in a cooperative and constructive manner.

It's a politics aware that all of our challenges are compounded by the addition *weekly* of about 1,500,000 people to our global population.

Business

In business and commerce, our old way of thinking is about short-term gain.

It's about maximizing profit in the short-term.

People and our environment are exploited.

Our emerging worldview is about long-term gain and sustainability.

It's socially responsible business.

It's about a triple bottom line: people, planet, and profit.

It's the enlightened understanding that life is a far more complex phenomenon than a race to see who can accumulate the most.

Social Interaction

In social interaction, the old worldview is focused on us versus them.

It's about exclusivity and segregation.

The emerging worldview is about inclusiveness, integration, oneness, togetherness, and assimilation.

Religion

Old religious thought is about my truth and tribe versus your truth and tribe.

The result is never ending conflict and chaos, the antithesis of peace.

The emerging worldview, whatever the religion, emphasizes kindness and universal benevolence.

It thinks intelligently about the origins of ancient religions and the phenomenon of religion itself.

In summary, our *old worldview* is characterized by separation, exclusivity, segregation, and unilateralism.

Our *emerging worldview* is about togetherness, unity, inclusiveness, integration, and multilateralism.

Many of us are predisposed as a consequence of our genetics and/or our life experiences to think and act in our old, destructive and unsustainable ways.

This requires unlearning and evolution of thought and behavior, all of which are daunting challenges.

The new way of thinking is one that requires learning.

What is it that we must learn?

We must learn that we exist as a tiny fragment of an immensely larger interlocking whole in which all of the parts are interconnected and dependent upon each other for survival.

— *Part III - The Solution* —

Simply put, everything is connected to everything else.
We exist not separately but in communion with all living things.
Life is an interrelated interdependent phenomenon.
That is the nature of the web of life.
That is the nature of the reality in which we exist.

Reality has behavioral demands.

These can be summarized in seven interrelated words which form three simple rules for living:

Be healthy.
Be kind.
Respect the environment.

These seven words have the power to change the way we govern, the laws that we enact, the way we do business, the products that we create, the services that we offer, how we treat our employees, our environment, each other, and ourselves.

Be healthy.
Be kind.
Respect the environment.

Leaders must model this behavior.
Teachers must teach it.
We must exhibit it . . . if we wish to sustain humanity and advance our civilization.
To do so requires entering into a completely new understanding of the reality in which we exist.

Our window of opportunity to make the necessary and monumental shift in thinking is small compared to the large obstacles in our current belief systems that must be dissolved.
Yet, we must do this if we and all the life forms that share this jewel of a planet are to survive.

Be healthy.
Be kind.
Respect the environment.

Why are these seven words so critical and powerful?

Because we exist as a tiny fragment of an immensely larger *interlocking whole*—the operative words—in which all the parts are interconnected and dependent upon each other for survival.

We exist not separately but in communion with all living things.

This interlocking whole is the undeniable foundation for the architecture of life and our civilization.

If we continue to destroy the relationships that form this foundation (relationships with our health, each other, and our environment), our house, our structure, our civilization will disintegrate and, eventually, collapse.

Conversely, if we honor these relationships, we will succeed and prosper in every way.

The choice is ours.
Our future lies in our own hands.
It always has.

The difference today is that we understand a great deal more about what sustains and optimizes life.

It is time to honor the knowledge that we have and act in a sustainable manner.

It's time for humanity to grow up.

Only then, will we improve the quality of our lives, arrest and reverse our destructive and unsustainable momentum, end our needless suffering, prosper together, find peace, sustain humanity, and advance our civilization.

GROUNDED IN REALITY

We have an opportunity and a responsibility to correct errors that began thousands of years ago in the infancy of our intelligence.

We did not then understand what is truly sacred.

Instead of recognizing the sacredness in life all around us, we created and worshipped fictional gods.

Many of us, albeit less and less, still do.

We created these fictional supernatural beings long before the Scientific Revolution and the Enlightenment (the Age of Reason) to explain the mysteries of life and to provide us with the courage to face life's challenges and tragedies.

Over time, we transformed fiction into "fact" and forfeited our power to these deities.

We then wove a web of deceit to respond to every logical challenge to our own contrived stories.

This deceit and delusion continue today.

With the knowledge we have, *it is long past time* to let go of this ancient fiction.

It's time to get grounded in reality and honor that which is clearly sacred here and now.

There are no saviors that will come to our rescue.

It's just us.

Only we can save ourselves.

What is sacred here and now is that which at our peril we cannot violate, damage, dishonor, or destroy.

It has nothing to do with gods, religions, or anything supernatural.

We cannot violate our health.

We cannot violate people.

We cannot violate our environment.

Unless we wish to suffer.

We have everything we require on this spaceship we call Earth to create a splendid world and fulfilling lives.//
In order to thrive, all life forms must align with that which supports and sustains life.//
To do so means to be responsible for our health, be kind to others, and respect our environment.//
That's the simple truth.

The large number of people who have abandoned and continue to leave antiquated religions is profound, understandable, and a sign of progress.//
The trend will continue.

It's been said that there is nothing as powerful as an idea whose time has come.//
The reverse is true: there is nothing as weak as an idea whose time has passed.//
That's what's going on in the world of our inherited ancient religions.//
They are being abandoned.//
Their time has passed.

— *Part III - The Solution* —

I saw this development to be inevitable many years ago when I studied at Harvard Divinity School.

In polls, the reasons for quitting religion vary to include rejection of one's childhood faith, antipathy toward organized religion, and negative personal experiences with religion.

From my perspective, the abandonment of religion is also a consequence of our age of information and communication.

The close examination of religion afforded to anyone today, which in the past was not possible, translates into ongoing declines for these ancient dinosaurs and, for many, eventual extinction.

The children of the future will look incredulously at how long into the modern era these primitive religions held power, influence, and followers.

For good reason, many people are alarmed and fearful of the multiple challenges humanity, with its ever-expanding population, faces.

Most people today seek answers to life's challenges here and now in reality.

Not in some afterlife.

Not from supernatural sources.

That's a positive development that is essential if we are to sustain humanity and advance our civilization.

Species come and go.

Only if humanity changes its ways will it survive.

Otherwise humanity will continue to be mired in unnecessary, debilitating, and worsening problems.

The empirical evidence is that change often comes, not from enlightenment but, from crises.

Enlightenment often comes from crises as well.

A crisis is life's way of telling us it's time for a change.

We have many crises on our planet.

We are in a position to learn much if we pay attention and respond appropriately.

Life is always teaching; we're not always listening and learning.

When a crisis occurs, one of two things happens.

One, the crisis is ignored.

This results in tragic, often terminal, consequences.

Or second, the crisis is a wakeup call.

Changes are made, the crisis is averted, and incremental improvement begins.

This is true for individuals, and groups of individuals as small as marriages to as large as nation states and civilizations.

While it is true that we learn from crises, it is also true that we can learn from observing the crises of others.

We do not have to experience crises ourselves to learn their lessons.

Humanity can learn from virtual crises that we can project with our current knowledge and technologies.

Humanity can act while the crises are in their early stages and stop their advance.

Humanity is challenged always to evolve and improve.

The Time Has Come

The time has come to abandon our primitive instincts and behavior.

The time has come to feed people's hope, not their hate.

The time has come to move beyond the use of force to settle our differences.

— *Part III - The Solution* —

The time has come when the destruction of any living species is no longer acceptable and will no longer be tolerated.

The time has come for us to advance beyond antiquated and divisive religions to a world grounded in reality.

The time has come to appreciate that our planet exists within a very narrow band in our solar system that enables life to flourish.

The time has come for the people of Earth, with unprecedented inclusiveness, respect for diversity, and a sense of responsibility for the whole of life to join together and move humanity and civilization in a direction that is peaceful, just, and sustainable.

Be healthy.
Be kind.
Respect the environment.

DECLARATION OF HUMANITY

IT IS TIME

Our hunger for peace and security compels us to launch a new era in human history.

We have the knowledge and technological means to reduce ignorance and suffering and to expand knowledge and justice.

It is within our powers to restore our planet, sustain humanity, and advance our civilization.

We can bequeath to posterity a beautiful planetary home in which all people enjoy a more peaceful and healthy life.

Our world is fraught with grotesque economic disparities, life-threatening and accelerating environmental damage, violence of all manner and scale, and immeasurable suffering.

The very institutions we have organized to guarantee our security and survival too often produce the opposite results.

Our politics are adversarial and ineffective, our industries' toll on our natural systems is unsustainable, and our religious thought—dated and dogmatic—divides rather than joins us.

Our always growing world population compounds and complicates our problems.

The needs, demands, and desires of humanity exceed the sustainable yields of our natural systems.

We have set into motion complex and destructive processes that we do not fully understand, that have consequences beyond our ability to define and, at some point, could reach destructive levels beyond our ability to control.

We are the victims of our own behavior.

We've created an unsustainable momentum that must be arrested and reversed.

If we are to improve the quality of our lives, sustain humanity, and advance our civilization, it is required that we enter into a new way to understand and relate to reality.

Our window of opportunity to accomplish this necessary and monumental shift is small compared to the large obstacles within our current belief systems that must be dissolved.

Yet, we must do this if we and all the life forms that share this jewel of a planet are to survive.

We do not have time or resources to continue to treat each other as adversaries or to further exploit and destroy our environment.

We are weary of humanity's epic and horrific struggles that, as individuals, we experience and witness daily.

Many of us share the belief that humanity and its institutions must evolve and respond appropriately to the life-sustaining demands of reality.

The natural course of human evolution reveals vital and timeless truths that await discovery.

One such truth has emerged in our lifetime.

It informs us that we exist as a tiny fragment of an immensely larger interlocking whole in which all of the parts are interconnected and dependent upon each other for survival.

Simply put, everything is connected.

— *Declaration of Humanity* —

Humans exist not separately, but in communion with all living things.

Life is an interrelated interdependent phenomenon.

If we continue to live unhealthy lives, damage and destroy our relationships with each other and our environment, all of which form the foundation of our existence, our civilization will disintegrate and, in time, collapse.

Conversely, if we honor these relationships, we will succeed and prosper in every way.

The choice is ours.

Our fate lies in our own hands as it always has.

Today, however, we understand far more about what sustains and optimizes life.

It is time to honor and apply the knowledge that we have.

Only then, will we arrest and reverse our destructive and unsustainable momentum, end our needless suffering, prosper together, find peace, sustain humanity, and advance our civilization.

- As life is far more complex than a race to see who can accumulate the most, **commerce** must, above all, be grounded in respect for people and our environment.

It is time.

- As we have severe, urgent, and complicated global and local problems that must be addressed cooperatively and constructively and do not have the time, resources, and energy to squander fighting with each other as individuals or nation states, **politics** must, above all, and with unequivocal urgency, find common ground.

It is time.

- As the ancient mentality of "my truth and tribe versus your truth and tribe" has resulted in nothing but interminable conflict and chaos, **religious thought** must, above all, support universal benevolence and be grounded in and revere reality.

It is time.

- As exclusivity and segregation have served only to separate us superficially, **social interaction** must, above all, be inclusive and integrated as to mirror the interconnected phenomenon and structure of life itself.

It is time.

We are each a cell in the body of humanity.

The physical, mental, and emotional health each of us brings to our world determines our collective health and wholeness.

It is time to find comfort in our own individuality, joy in our relationships with each other, and respect for our environment.

These are the dictates of the reality of our existence.

Our behavior must be characterized not by short-term survival instincts—like fear, greed, power, control, immediate gratification, self-centeredness, authoritarianism, and denial of inequality—but by health in all of its dimensions, kindness toward each other and other nation states, and reverence for our life-sustaining environment and the web of life.

It matters not how much wealth we have, what size home(s) we possess, what kind of vehicles we own, how many academic degrees

— *Declaration of Humanity* —

we have accumulated, what achievements we may have accomplished, or what is our title or position.

Nor does it matter our gender, race, religion, age, appearance, national origin, sexual orientation, or political affiliation.

What matters is whether or not we are kind to one another.
In the final analysis, in every way conceivable, we are linked to our environment.
We are one people bound together and dependent upon one body of natural resources.

If we destroy our environment, we destroy ourselves.
In time, damaged ecological systems will regenerate but we will be gone.
Nature, which could not care less, will have eliminated us.

While it is true that we have free will to act as we please, in an interrelated interdependent world the consequences are fixed.
Our only choices are, in fact, to honor that which sustains and optimizes life and prosper together in peace or violate that which sustains and optimizes life and suffer together in turmoil.

Our common destiny and sense of survival summons us to evolve and advance toward our higher potential.
Nature will go its own course with or without us.
Our course depends upon our choices.

Let us, as individuals and organizations, bring forth a more compassionate, peaceful, cooperative, and secure humanity.

Let the following define the legacy of our time.

- That we acknowledge the essential oneness of humanity and life in all its diverse expressions.

- That we revere life, support universal benevolence, and insist upon sustainable industry.

- That we support an equitable sharing of the Earth's resources.

- That we commit to the reduction of ignorance, illiteracy, hunger, poverty, and disease.

- That we seek and support a compassionate and just society.

- That we demand that our planetary resources be restored and sustained.

- That we support unprecedented international cooperation.

At this time in the evolution of humanity, all of this is within our perception and grasp.

IT IS TIME

AUTHOR

Joseph R. Simonetta holds a Master of Architecture degree from the University of Colorado. He also studied architecture at the University of Southern California.

He holds a Master of Divinity degree from Harvard Divinity School. He also studied at Yale Divinity School.

He holds a B.S. in Business Logistics from Penn State University.

Born November 22, 1943 in a World War II housing project in Bethlehem, Pennsylvania, he is the second of three sons of an immigrant blue-collar steelworker and his wife.

He was raised in the shadows of the blast furnaces of the Bethlehem Steel Corporation.

He has since lived for significant amounts of time in California, Colorado, Massachusetts, Connecticut, Florida, Greece, New Zealand, and Ecuador.

His rich life experiences encompass many fields.

He has been an Army officer, professional athlete, entrepreneur and businessman, architect, real estate developer, home builder, environmental activist, author, senior editor of the World Business Academy, twice a nominee for the U.S. Congress, and once a nominee for the U.S. presidency (Democratic Party National Convention, New York City, 1992).

This book is based on his lecture series, "Astonish the World, Tell the Simple Truth."

He is married to Susana Rojas Simonetta.

They have a son, Russell, born April 22, 2013 (Earth Day), and a daughter, Fiorella, born October 12, 2015.

Made in the USA
Columbia, SC
22 December 2020